MESSY PROGRESS

I0155311

Crying. Coping. Carrying on.

SRUTI MISHRA

ink Scribe

ink

Messy Progress

Copyright © 2025 Sruti Mishra

Publisher: Inkscribe Publishing Pvt. Ltd.

ISBN Number: 978-1-969259-01-2

Contents

Note for Reader

Dear Reader,

If you're holding this book, chances are — you're a little tired.
Maybe tired of trying so hard.
Maybe tired of being strong.
Maybe tired of not knowing where you're headed, or why everyone else seems so sure.

Maybe you're just trying to keep it together. Aren't we all?
Everyone's learning something. Everyone's got their own mess—some just hide it better.

Let me start by saying this: *You're not alone.*

This book wasn't written by an expert in motivation or a polished life coach. It was written by someone who knows what it's like to sit in a classroom feeling invisible. To carry pressure that feels too heavy for your age. To smile in public and quietly fall apart in private.
To try — and still not feel like enough.

Messy Progress is a love letter to students — not just the ones in school, but the ones still learning how to live. The ones who overthink, compare, dream differently, cry quietly, and keep showing up anyway. Whether you're 18 or 38, if you've ever felt lost in a world of achievers, this book is for you.

You don't have to read it in order. You don't have to finish it in one sitting.
Read a page when you feel like giving up.
Reread a line when you need someone to say, *"I get it."*

I'm not here to fix you. Honestly, I'm still figuring out mine.
I'm here to remind you — *you don't need fixing.*

You're allowed to feel messy. And still grow.
You're allowed to not have it all together. And still move forward.
You're allowed to be a learner — forever.

With Love,
Sruti

You Are Not Alone If...

- You've laughed in a group chat but felt completely invisible.
- You've kept typing, then deleting, then typing again — and still never hit send.
- You've smiled when you actually wanted to disappear.
- You've told people you're fine just so they'd stop asking.
- You've scored well and still felt worthless.
- You've felt jealous of people who aren't even happy.
- You've watched everyone clap for someone else and wondered if anyone would ever clap for you.
- You've felt like the only one not moving forward.
- You've blamed yourself for not being "normal" enough.
- You've wondered if anyone would ever understand you completely.

If you nodded —
Congrats, you're a human. Not a robot.
Write down what you've been carrying. No one's watching.
Then turn the page.
This book's not here to fix you.
It's here to say: *same pinch !*

Write the thing you've never admitted — not even to yourself.

The Race I Never Signed Up For

I don't remember the exact day it started. Maybe it was the first time someone leaned over and asked, "How many marks did you get?"

Or maybe it was when the teacher announced the topper's name, and a small wave of claps echoed in the classroom, while the rest of us looked down, tying imaginary shoelaces, pretending we didn't care.

Suddenly, life wasn't just about learning anymore. It became a performance. A scoreboard. A ranking.

It became a race — a quiet one, without a starting gun or a map, and definitely no idea of the finish line. Just a strange feeling that you needed to run. Always. And somehow, you were already behind.

The Race Didn't Just Start in School. It Started in Nursery.

Believe it or not, the first race was over who could identify colors the fastest. Then it turned into who could recite A for Apple to Z for Zebra without messing up the middle. And of course, who got a star sticker that day.

Those little gold stars? They were our first medals.

If you brought home five, your parents smiled. If you brought home none, they asked, "What happened today?" — as if the absence of a sticker meant the presence of failure.

That's when we first learned: **doing well = being praised**, and being praised felt like safety.

And so we ran.

The Pencil Box

Yes, it's a thing. And if you were a student in any classroom post-1990s, you know what I'm talking about.

One kid brought a pencil box with two layers and a pop-up sharpener. The next day, another upgraded to one with a calculator. By the end of the week, someone had one with a *secret drawer* with a colourful small pen inside it.

Suddenly, your perfectly functional pencil box looked like an early man's weapon from ancient times.

And that's how you learned the earliest lesson of capitalism: **Comparison kills joy.**

You didn't need a new one. But you *wanted* it. Because if they had it, and you didn't — maybe they were ahead, and you were falling behind.

Fitting In

By middle school, it wasn't just about grades anymore. Recess had its own politics.

Some friends were into cricket stats. Some could quote anime dialogues. Some were dancers. Some were into Starplus serials. And some were the quiet readers who always had a book in hand (and low-key intimidated everyone else).

Maybe by then you had no idea where you fit in. Maybe you tried laughing at jokes you didn't get. Or nodding along to conversations about shows you never watched. Just to avoid being that person who sat alone.

Fitting in became a race too.

Not for survival. But for acceptance.

So you shapeshifted. You became the funny one. Or the silent one. Or the "chill" one who didn't care (but definitely did). You became a version of yourself that felt easier to like — even if it didn't feel like *you*.

The Morning Assembly Awards

Oh, how those moments lived rent-free in our heads.

"Today, we're proud to announce the winners of the inter-school debate competition..."

Even if you clapped, you might have felt a small knot form inside you. A whisper: "Should I have participated? Why didn't I? What's wrong with me?"

Every achievement by someone else somehow felt like a failure of your own. Even if you weren't interested in debating or dancing.

That's the cruelty of the race — **it makes you want trophies you didn't even want.**

Report Card Days

There's nothing quite like the tension of walking home with a sealed report card.

Step 1: Don't open it.
Step 2: Open it anyway.
Step 3: Stare at the marks like they're someone else's.
Step 4: Think of excuses. Not reasons — excuses.
Step 5: Hope your sibling did worse. (You know it's messed up. Still.)
Step 6: Practice your face. Neutral. Not too sad. Not too chill.

Because it's not just marks.
It's whether your parents talk to you with love tonight — or just with disappointment.
It's whether you're "focused" or "a problem."
It's whether they say "it's okay" or bring up Sharma ji again.

You laugh it off with friends. But deep down, it burns.
Because you wanted to do well too.
You just didn't.
And now, that number decides if you're good enough — for the next few months, or maybe longer.

And the worst part?
You start believing it too.

You vs. Everyone Else

By college, the race got new names: placements, internships, career plans.

"Where are you applying?"
"Do you have a backup?"
"Startups are in, you know."

Everyone looked like they had a LinkedIn strategy. You still struggled to finish your résumé.

It wasn't about just being good anymore — it was about being *better than everyone else.*

Better portfolio.
Better university.
Better smile in your convocation picture.

And the finish line kept moving.

The Emotional Aftertaste of Racing

The problem with being in a race you didn't sign up for is — you don't get to stop and breathe.

Even your hobbies start to feel like competitions.
Even your breaks feel like laziness.
Even your peace starts to feel like guilt.

And slowly, you forget what you even liked doing.
What you even wanted.
Who you were before this all began.

Still Running, Barefoot, In the Wrong Direction ?

If this feels familiar…
You're not alone.

We've all, at some point, tried to outpace people we didn't even like, to win prizes we didn't even want.
We've confused speed with growth.
We've mistaken applause for belonging.

But maybe the real learning starts when we slow down.
When we pause and say:
"I don't want to run anymore. Not like this."

At that point, you're not behind. You're not failing.
You're just becoming.
At your pace.

On your path.
And that's the only race worth running.

But here's the funny part —
Most of us are still out here running half-hearted marathons with full-blown confusion.
Some with timetables.
Some with trauma.
And some with a tiffin box in one hand, and identity crisis in the other.

We entered races just because the crowd was moving.
Didn't even check what sport it was.
Turns out, half of us are swimming in the wrong pool. Fully clothed.

And still wondering — "Why am I tired all the time?"

So here's a thought:
Not every race needs your participation.
Not every starting line deserves your shoes.

Run the ones that light you up, not the ones that burn you out.
Because if you're going to be breathless anyway —
Might as well be for something you actually give a damn about.

Because running blindly might make you fast -
But running wisely makes you free.

When Everyone's Ahead

Let's get brutally honest — comparison sucks.

One moment, you're living your life, just minding your own slightly chaotic business, and the next thing you know, someone posts their promotion, engagement, abs, book launch, destination wedding, and homemade Dahi Bhalle on Instagram — all before 9 AM.

You're sitting there in a blanket , staring at that chair full of both clean and used clothes and a to-do list that's been gathering emotional dust for three weeks. And you think, "Everyone's moving ahead like life gave them clarity, and I'm here second-guessing my every step, dressing up confusion as 'patience'."

This chapter is about the ache that creeps in when you start to feel like you're the only one not thriving. The Comparison Trap. Or the emotional version of "Scrolling Through Lives That Left Me Behind."

Different Flavors of Jealousy: A Lifelong Menu

Jealousy is an equal opportunity emotion — no age bar, no dress code. It's for *everyone*.
You, me, your therapist, your dog — hell, even monks probably get jealous of the other monk's enlightenment glow.

Because jealousy isn't about hate.
It's about *lack*.
It's about the sting of watching someone live a version of life you didn't even know you wanted — until it showed up on your feed with filters, hashtags, and 2K likes.

So yeah, let's stop pretending we're above it.

1. Nursery Jealousy:

Your favourite teacher smiled at someone else and said, "You're my little smartie."
You stood there blinking, your coloring half-done, your heart full of questions no toddler should have.
You didn't know the word for it, but your body knew.
That weird, heavy feeling in your chest. The way you suddenly didn't want to show her your drawing anymore.
You thought *you* were special. Until you weren't.
And that was your first lesson in how fragile affection can feel — even when you're still learning the alphabet.

2. Primary School Jealousy:

You opened your tiffin and saw cold roti with aloo sabzi. Again.
Your benchmate had Oreos, Frooti, and Maggi in a steel dabba that somehow looked more luxurious than a five-star buffet.
He offered to share. You smiled. Said no.
Because it wasn't about the food. It was about what the food *meant*.
You were too young to say it, but a part of you whispered:
"Why don't I get the good stuff?"
You didn't want a snack — you wanted to feel *chosen*. Loved in a way that looked like shiny packets and lunchbox envy.

3. High School Jealousy:

You saw your crush laugh with that one girl. The girl who always knew the answers. Who always smelled like fresh shampoo and confidence.
He passed her a pen. Just a pen.
But something in you cracked.
You smiled, acted cool, but mentally you were already watching them fall in love, get married, and maybe name their first kid.
And then you went home and played *"Tujhe yaad na meri aayi"* on loop while pretending not to care.
Because no one tells you that teenage jealousy isn't rage.
It's grief.
Grief for a love story that only existed in your imagination.

4. College Jealousy:

You sat in the front row. You studied when no one else did. You overachieved.
They didn't even buy the textbook.

But they got the dream internship — and you got politely ghosted after your 3rd follow-up email.
You smiled through it. Said, *"Good for them."*
But at night, staring at your cracked phone screen, you thought:
"Why do I always have to try so hard just to be average?"
You didn't hate them. You hated how easy it looked for everyone else.
And how invisible your effort felt in a world built for loud wins and quiet losses.

Workplace Jealousy:

You've been in this job long enough to know everyone's coffee order and trauma.
Then one day, the new intern speaks in a meeting, and suddenly they're "a future leader."
You nod. You smile. You even say, "Wow, good point."
But inside, you're thinking, *"If I vanished tomorrow, would anyone even change the team group name?"*
You're not asking for a parade. Just maybe some credit, a name pronounced correctly, and a manager who doesn't start every sentence with "Quick favour?"
Because when you give your whole self to a place and still feel invisible, the jealousy isn't loud.
It's quiet.
It hides in the spaces between "sure, I'll take care of it" and *"I'm fine."*

Adulting Jealousy:

Someone just had a baby.
Someone else just bought a house with a balcony.
And you?
You just changed your bedsheet for the first time in two weeks.
You're not jealous of the baby or the house — you're jealous of the *certainty*. The stability.
Because you're still out here splitting rent with people who label their milk, surviving one HR call away from quitting, and nursing yet another heartbreak from someone who said *"I'm not ready for anything serious"* but still texted you at 2 a.m.
You don't even want a baby.
You just want to stop crying every time you see a wedding post, a housewarming invite, or a couple who actually buys groceries *together*.
Adulthood, you thought, would feel like a warm bed.
But mostly, it feels like trying to fall asleep in the cold with a noisy brain and someone else's Spotify ad playing in the background.

Let's not sugarcoat it — jealousy is just 'just' emotionally mature code for *"Why the hell not me?"*

But here's the thing: jealousy isn't about them.
It's a flashlight aimed directly at your own unmet needs and abandoned dreams.
It shows you where you feel small, where you feel stuck, and where you secretly think you're failing.
Not because you are — but because some outdated version of you expected you'd be a goddamn superhero by now.

The worst part?
Jealousy never shows up alone.
Nope. It brings its messy roommates — **insecurity, self-doubt,** and **shame** — who eat all your snacks and play *"What's Wrong With You?"* on loop at 2 a.m.

Insecurity

Why: Jealousy is the loud toddler; insecurity is the tired parent behind it. It's that exhausting whisper of "You're not enough."

How it shows up:
"Her handwriting looked like fonts. Mine looked like anxiety attacks."
"Maybe I'm not meant to shine. Some people glow. I glitch."

You ever rehearse a sentence in your head 10 times and still say it weird? That's insecurity holding the mic.

Self-Doubt

Why: Comparison makes you question yourself, even if no one else is. It's not jealousy of them — it's rejection of you.

How it shows up:

- "She didn't even try. I tried so hard I forgot why I started."
- "Even when I won, I wondered if it was just pity or luck."

You gaslight your own victories. Even success feels suspicious.

Shame

Why: Jealousy is painful. Shame is the layer that says, "You don't deserve to feel this."

How it shows up:

- "I clapped louder than anyone. That way no one would hear the tantrum in my throat."
- "I muted her stories. Not because I hated her. But because I hated who I became while watching them."

And let's be honest — we've all done the fake laugh, the overly supportive comment, the 'I'm so happy for you' that felt like chewing glass.

A Feed That Feeds Your Doubts:

You open Instagram.
Promotions. Pregnancies. Prettier lives.
Everyone's glowing.
You're just... logged in, hoping the algorithm throws you a bone of validation.

But here's what the post never tells you:
Behind that vacation was a fight.
Behind the degree, a breakdown.
Behind the wedding photo, a thousand doubts and maybe even a sleeping pill.
Behind the baby, a miscarriage no one could talk about.
Behind the house, debt that keeps them up at night.

We envy, then hate ourselves for envying.
We compare, then shame ourselves for not rising above it.

May be, jealousy is not a sin, it's a signal. a signal saying, ' There's something inside you still waiting to be lived'.

The Screaming Reminder That You Give a Damn

Jealousy isn't polite.
It doesn't knock.
It barges in — heart racing, hands clenched — dragging up everything you once wanted but buried.
Or worse, something brand new you'd die to have... but never dared to name.

It makes you flinch at someone else's joy.
It makes you question if the timeline you're on even leads anywhere worth arriving at.
It makes you hate people you love — just for living a version of the life you silently ache for.

But here's what we never say out loud:

Jealousy doesn't visit the hopeless.
It visits the ones who still *believe*.
Who still feel the thrum of a life unlived, just beneath the noise.

It's not about *their* glow-up.
It's about *your* hunger.
Not about the house they bought or the milestones they flaunt —
But about the version of you you've kept on hold.

And maybe that's the truth jealousy came to tell.

It's not evil.
It's not some shameful flaw to be purged.
It's the heartbeat under the hurt — the proof that something inside you is still alive and waiting.

The wake up call in the dark whispering:

"There's still a life in you that wants to be lived."

Let that ache crack you open.
Let it sting.
Let it lead.

Because if it didn't matter, you wouldn't feel it.

And it *does*.
You *do*.

Motivation Doesn't Live Here Anymore

———— ❧ ————

One day you wake up.
But you don't.

Your eyes open, sure.
Your legs swing off the bed.
But *you* — the part of you that gave a damn — is still somewhere under the sheets.

You sit on the edge of the bed, staring at nothing and everything.
Scrolling. Blinking. Scrolling.
The world's moving, glowing, hustling — and you're just... buffering.

It's not sadness. Not exactly. Not even depression, maybe.
It's this weird, weightless nothing.
Like you're alive, but unplugged. Present, but not participating.
It's like your brain is a room someone left in a rush — drawers open, coffee still warm, but no one home.
And every notification feels like a mosquito in that empty room — buzzing with someone else's productivity, someone else's glow-up, someone else's day that somehow *started*.

Meanwhile, you're sitting there negotiating with your willpower like:
"Okay, we'll shower... but only if we can lie back down immediately after."
You laugh at yourself. But not really.

You're not lazy. You are not sleep-deprived. You're just... unrecovered.

You're tired in a way that no sleep can fix.
Tired from holding it all together for so long that "trying" has become a full-time performance, the kind of performance that should not stop.

And now?
Even trying feels fake.
Like signing up for another hustle you already know will leave you empty.

Motivation didn't vanish just that way.
It got tired of begging.
Tired of knocking on a door that never got answered because you were too busy pretending everything was fine.

And no—don't say you lost your spark.

You didn't lose it.
You *spent* it.
Trying to keep everything running.
Trying to be okay.
Trying to light the way for others while your own match burned down to the fingers.

Fake Energy. Real Exhaustion.

You learn how to fake it.
The smile. The "Haha, I'm fine."
The energy that looks like motivation but is really just social pressure wearing sunglasses.

You show up. Because you have to.
You speak in meetings. You reply to texts. You laugh at memes.
And on the outside, you look… functional.

But inside? You're scraping the bottom.
Of patience. Of hope. Of whatever tiny voice used to say, *"Come on, we've got this."*

There are no breakdowns, no sobbing on the floor.
Just a quiet, steady leaking of your will to try.

You used to want more — to build, to become, to matter.
Now you just want a day where nothing is demanded from you.
A day where you're allowed to just… *be* without apologizing for it.

But you can't say that out loud, right?
So you keep playing the part.
Nodding. Smiling. "Doing great."

And everyone believes you.
Because you're good at pretending.
Because it's easier for them if you are.

But you know the truth.

There's a cost to pretending.
And you've been paying it in silence, in sleep, in your ability to feel joy without checking how productive it looks.

You don't need more caffeine.
You need permission to stop performing energy you don't have.

Because this isn't just exhaustion.
It's grief for the version of you *who used to be excited to live*.

The Cost of Pretending

(and the slow grief of losing yourself)

Pretending doesn't break you all at once.
It doesn't explode — it erodes.
Tiny moments, everyday betrayals of your own energy.

It starts with "I'm just tired."
Then becomes "I'll bounce back soon."
And one day, without warning, it turns into
"I don't remember who I was before this version of me started performing survival."

You keep showing up — for work, for calls, for people —
but not for yourself.
Because the version of you that used to get excited, that used to dream without caution —
is now archived somewhere under 'maybe later.'

And the grief?
It's not loud.
It's not cinematic.
It's quiet and constant, like background noise you've forgotten how to mute.

You grieve the you who used to laugh freely.
The one who believed rest didn't have to be earned.
The one who wasn't always measuring their worth in output.

But you can't tell anyone you're grieving someone who's technically still alive.

So you keep going.
Keep producing.
Keep nodding.
While somewhere deep inside, a softer voice whispers,
"This isn't what we wanted. This isn't who we are."

And that ache —
that quiet ache of misalignment —
isn't laziness.
It's the soul's way of saying: *You've been missing from your own life.*

Nothing Feels Enough

(Because you're not chasing goals — you're chasing permission to breathe.)

You did everything they said would make you feel fulfilled.
You showed up. You pushed through. You became "reliable."
You were the strong one. The sorted one. The one who never breaks.

And now?
You're exhausted in a way no weekend can fix.

You get the praise.
The raise.
The occasional "How do you do it all?"

But deep inside, some part of you mutters:

"Why doesn't anything feel like it's mine?"

You look around your life like a house you once built and now live in as a tenant.
Well-decorated. Functional.
But not home.

And here's where it gets brutally human:
When survival becomes your personality, peace feels like laziness.
You start to think maybe you don't *deserve* ease — not until you've earned it through a little more pain.

So you keep running.
From the silence.

From the stillness.
From the truth.

Because stopping would mean facing the version of you that's quietly bleeding under all that productivity.

But here's the twist — that version?
That tired, burnt-out, joy-hungry version?
They don't need a pep talk.

They need mercy.

The Ending: Where Mercy Begins

No one tells you how often we abandon ourselves.

Not dramatically.
Not in some tragic, cinematic, walking-away-in-the-rain way.
But quietly.
Repeatedly.
In small, invisible betrayals.

When we say "yes" just to be liked.
When we shrink so others don't feel small.
When we stay, smile, nod — even when we're quietly bleeding under the skin.

We don't need enemies.
We've got ourselves.
Tearing down our worth with the same hands that built the façade.

And here's the part that guts you the most:
The person who has suffered most from your silence, your perfectionism, your burnout?

It's not your parents.
Not your ex.
Not your job.
Not the world.

It's you.
You paid the full price for being everyone's solution but your own.

So here's a wild, radical, inconvenient idea:
What if you didn't fix yourself right now?
What if you didn't set another goal or download another productivity app or fake
another "I'm doing great!"?

What if — stay with me here —
you just gave yourself *mercy*?

Not the fluffy kind.
Not the Instagram-quote kind.
The real kind.
The kind that looks like crying in your parked car and not shaming yourself for it.
The kind that cancels plans and doesn't write a thesis on why.
The kind that says, *"I'm not okay. But I still deserve love anyway."*

Because maybe — just maybe —
healing isn't a grand staircase.
Maybe it's just *pausing the performance long enough*
to hear the part of you that's still whispering: *"Please... don't give up on me too."*

And that, right there, is where the next chapter begins.
Not in discipline.
Not in productivity.
But in mercy.

The kind of mercy that feels like weakness...
until you realise it's the only reason you're still breathing.

The Fear of Being Average

You ever walk into a room and feel like the dumbest person there?
Not because anyone said it — they didn't need to.
It's in the way they casually drop book references you've never heard of.
It's in how easily they seem to belong, while you're still rehearsing your introduction in your head.

You tell a joke. They smile politely.
You share an idea. They nod, but their eyes are already scanning for someone else to talk to.
And suddenly, it's not just *a moment*.
It's an internal crisis.

Your brain says, *"Act normal."*
Your heart says, *"Run."*

Average feels like a slap — not because of failure,
but because of **how silently you've been trying**.
And no one notices.

It started early. You answered a few math problems faster than the kid next to you, and suddenly the adults decided you were different. Gifted. Destined. You were the chosen one ! By age ten, you were already carrying the weight of words like *potential*, *brilliance*, and *bright future*. Your only real accomplishment? Finishing homework without crying.

But it stuck. You believed it.
You were supposed to be something.
Something **more.**

But life doesn't care about the praises you got in fifth grade.
Life is unimpressed.

Because one day you grow up — and you're not the smartest in the room anymore. Hell, you're barely keeping up. And there's no medal for that. Just bills, browser tabs, and a pile of "You should be doing more" quietly building up inside your chest.

You were told you were meant to shine.
So why does it feel like you're flickering?

No one warned you that potential, when not fulfilled fast enough, starts rotting inside you. That it doesn't shout — it whispers: "You were supposed to be more."

The world didn't break you.
It just didn't clap the way they promised it would.

Now, mediocrity feels like betrayal. Not because it's bad, but because it wasn't part of the script. You were built up like a climax was guaranteed.
Spoiler: there wasn't.

The Curse of Potential

When "You can do anything" turns into "Why the hell aren't you doing everything?"

You had *potential*. God, didn't everyone tell you that?

Every teacher, every distant uncle, every random adult who saw you draw one decent sketch or score a 90 once — all of them repeated it like a prophecy:

"This one's going to make it big."

And for a while, that felt good. Like you were carrying some divine spark in your pocket.

But here's the twist no one tells you:

Potential is a burden in slow motion.

You don't feel it at first — because it hides inside compliments.
But as the years go by, and you're still figuring out where your charger is, let alone your life purpose, it starts to morph.

From "you're talented" to
"you've wasted your talent."

From "you're made for more" to
"is this really all you're doing?"

And the cruel part?
You start saying it to *yourself.*

That inner voice becomes your worst boss:
Always disappointed. Never satisfied. Constantly comparing your blooper reel to someone else's highlight story, with a motivational quote slapped on top like a Band-Aid on a bullet wound.

You start measuring your worth in productivity.
In LinkedIn updates.
In how many tabs you can keep open before your brain crashes harder than your browser.

And God forbid you take a nap —
because then comes the guilt.
The *I-could've-been-working-on-my-dream* guilt.
The *someone-my-age-wrote-a-book-and-I-just-ate-biscuits-for-lunch-again* guilt.

Here's the raw truth no one stitched on a throw pillow:

The curse of potential isn't that you don't have it.
It's that you're terrified you'll never live up to it.

That every moment of rest feels like regression.
That you'll always be two steps behind some invisible deadline.

And the worst part?
There's no final exam.
No certificate that says, "Congrats, you did enough."

The Spotlight Delusion

You want to be seen — but not like *that.*
Not the way where people zoom in on your voice cracks or notice the way your hands fidget when you're nervous.
Not the way where one wrong sentence becomes a character flaw.

You want recognition — the filtered kind. The kind that claps for your effort, skips your insecurities, and doesn't ask any follow-up questions.

You want to post your thoughts, your work, your life — but lowkey pray it doesn't blow up too much. Because then… you'll have to live up to it. Repeatedly. Publicly. And what if they find out that you're just… guessing half the time?

You want the applause without the pressure.
The stage without the spotlight.
The visibility without the vulnerability.

So you stay in this bizarre limbo — desperate to matter, but terrified to be fully known. You want people to say, *"You're special,"* but you flinch if they ever ask, *"How are you, really?"*

It's not vanity. It's not even ego. It's **fear disguised as ambition.** Because deep down, you're not sure if you want to be admired… or just not forgotten.

So you curate and crop and caption and shrink and shine — all at once.

And somewhere in that exhausting performance, you lose track of a basic question:

If we're so scared of being average…
What the hell are we trying to be?

Maybe I felt invisible without external validation.

Somewhere along the way, applause became oxygen.

Not actual approval — but the *notification*, the "well done!", the "you're going places!" that hits like dopamine on a dying phone battery.

You don't even know if you *like* what you're doing anymore.
You just like the feeling of being *seen* doing it.

You post the certificate. The smiling group photo. The accomplishment you barely felt because you were already worried about how many people would "react."

You've become the highlight reel curator of a life that sometimes feels like it's happening to someone else.

And when no one claps?

When no one messages "Proud of you!" or hearts your story?

You feel like you're disappearing. Like maybe *you* don't matter if it isn't mattering *to them*.

And yeah, it sounds dramatic. But it's not drama — it's survival in a world that made you believe that if you're not trending, you're invisible.

But here's the gut-punch:

You were never built to be watched all the time.
You were built to **be**.

To live. Quietly or loudly.
To fail. Messily.
To *exist* — not for someone else's applause, but for your own damn joy.

Because maybe "average" isn't invisibility. Maybe it's freedom.

Redefining Average

Let's just say it out loud:
Most of us *are* average.
Statistically. Mathematically. Spiritually. Existentially.
And no, that's not an insult. That's just... Earth being Earth.

But somehow, we were raised like *potential demigods*.
"Beta, you're born to change the world!"

We grew up thinking being *average* is some kind of curse.
Like you'll wake up one day surrounded by mediocre 'Hometown Sale' furniture and whispers of "Could've been something" echoing from your ceiling fan.

But let's reframe.

Average is not a failure.
It's not a prison.
It's a **starting point** — a canvas. A decent Wi-Fi signal. A quiet room to ask:
"Okay, what *do* I actually want?"

Because maybe you don't want to scale Everest.
Maybe you just want to make dinner , and watch your family praising 'perfectly' cooked Chicken on a Sunday night.
Maybe your version of legacy is *not* a TED Talk, but *being there when someone needs you*.

Maybe you don't want to be iconic.
Maybe you just want to be okay. And maybe... *that* is sacred.

See, *extraordinary* sounds sexy — until you realize it often comes with sleepless nights, imposter syndrome, and a fanbase that only loves the version of you that's always performing.

Meanwhile, **average is air.**
You don't notice it, but it's keeping you alive.
You don't need *more* air than the next person to feel worthy — you just need *enough* to breathe.

We've confused visibility with value.
Hype with happiness.
And somewhere in the chaos, we forgot that peace isn't always found in being exceptional — it's found in **being enough**, on your own weird little terms.

You don't have to light up the whole sky.
Maybe just light a corner of your world and sit there — warm, real, and human.

Average isn't the enemy.

In a world screaming for greatness, choosing to be peacefully, purposefully average... might just be the most rebellious thing you ever do.

I Don't Belong Here

Somewhere between laughing at the group joke you didn't get and rewriting the same sentence in your answer sheet for the fifth time, it hits you — *you're not confused, you're misplaced*. You keep showing up, nodding along, playing the part, and still — it feels like you're wearing someone else's skin. Tight in all the wrong places. You can't name it yet, can't point to a reason that would pass as "logical" in a group chat. You don't even remember when the pretending started. Just that one day, you laughed too hard at a joke that wasn't funny, agreed with an opinion that didn't feel like yours, nodded at a dream that didn't belong to you. And then it became a habit — blending in. Shrinking your edges. Picking the safe seat in the room. You didn't choose this place. Not really. You just… ended up here. Because someone said it was a good idea.

You didn't land here accidentally. You said yes. You followed the script.
Worked hard. Smiled politely. Played along.
And still, you feel like a guest in your own goddamn story.

It's not that everything is bad.
It's just that none of it feels like *you*.

You keep nodding, keep showing up, keep pretending. But somewhere inside, a tiny voice — the one you keep trying to sedate with caffeine and "gratitude" — whispers:
"You're in the wrong room."

And maybe you are.

The Mask Gets Heavy
The exhausting performance of belonging.

You didn't ask for the role.
But damn, you nailed the audition.
Now you're stuck in it.

The emotionally available friend. The reliable employee. The agreeable daughter. The "chill" partner. The resilient student.
Whoever they needed you to be — you shapeshifted, not out of courage, but out of survival.

But here's the problem with always holding it together:

Eventually, it starts holding you hostage.

And it's not the big things that break you.
It's the small ones.
Forgetting your headphones on a bad day.
Being left on "read" when you needed someone to say anything.
Smiling too hard for too long at people who didn't notice you.

This isn't burnout. This is misfit.

At first, you think you're just being dramatic.
A little out of sync. A bit moody. Maybe too sensitive.
So you drink more coffee, fake more smiles, and tell yourself, *"It's just a phase."*

But what if it's not?

What if it's not a phase?
What if you're not lost — you're just in the wrong goddamn movie, mouthing someone else's lines, hoping no one notices you don't know the plot?

When Misfit Isn't a Phase

At first, you think you're just having a weird week.
Offbeat. Out of sync. Socially buffering.

But then the weeks become months.
And the feeling doesn't pass — it parks. Right in the middle of your chest.

Everyone's talking, but it feels like you're watching a movie without subtitles.
You're nodding, smiling, laughing at the right moments —
but inside, you're screaming into a pillow only you can hear.

You start thinking maybe you're not just *in the wrong room* —
maybe you're in the wrong chapter, the wrong genre, hell, maybe even the wrong book.

You try harder.
You dress the part, talk the part, even buy the planner that influencers swear by.
But still — something feels counterfeit. Like you're doing a very average job at pretending to be someone else.

You owe it to yourself to know the difference.
Between burnout and disinterest.
Between misfit and mediocrity.
Between being lazy… and being *lost*.

Because pushing in the wrong direction isn't ambition.
It's self-abandonment in disguise.

Ask yourself —
You started this with your heart, didn't you?
So if it's bleeding now, what is it—burnout, boredom, or betrayal?
And if you gave it your best… and it *still* didn't work—
What exactly is it?

People say, *"This is just a phase."*
But what if it isn't?
What if you were never meant to belong here in the first place?

What if you're not broken…
just in an ecosystem that's allergic to your kind of 'real'?

You're not dramatic. You're just done.
Done performing.
Done folding yourself small enough to fit into spaces never meant for your edges.

Maybe you weren't meant to belong.
Maybe you were meant to break the script entirely.

Leaving Without a Map

You don't always leave with clarity.
Sometimes, you just leave because staying is starting to cost you parts of yourself you never agreed to give up.

You don't leave with a grand vision.
You leave because something inside you finally whispered,
"This is not it. This was never it."
And for the first time, you listened.

It's not the kind of exit you write essays about.
It's quiet. Unceremonious.
Like setting down a heavy bag after carrying it for years —
and realizing your hands still remember how to shake.

You don't know what comes next.
You barely know who you are without the thing you've been pretending to love.
But you do know this:

You're not failing.
You're not lost.
You're just telling the truth — and that's what makes it feel like breaking.

Sometimes, walking away isn't weakness.
It's wisdom — disguised as exhaustion.

And maybe the only map you ever needed was the moment you said,
"I don't know where I'm going yet, but I can finally say where I can't stay."

Because *not belonging* isn't failure — it's information.
And sometimes, the most powerful thing you can do for your future
is to stop betraying yourself in the present.

The Space Between No and Yes

It's strange — this place you're in.

You've said no.
To the job. The person. The pressure. The pretending.
But you haven't said yes yet.

You're not running anymore, but you're not arriving either.

You're just... here.

And for the first time, that doesn't feel like failure.
It feels like *clearing*.

Like dust finally settling after years of rushing through days you didn't even like.
Like an inner voice — once drowned in the noise — finally whispering,
"You're not lost. You're just in the part of the story where you pause before the
chapter that changes everything."

This is the space where you unlearn hustle and re-learn healing.
Where you stop asking "what should I do?"
and start asking
"what feels like peace when no one's watching?"

It's quiet here.
Uncomfortable, sometimes.
But that's what growing out of your old life sounds like.

You're not broken.
You're just shedding the version of you that was built to survive, not thrive.

You're not behind.
You're just no longer willing to rush toward things that weren't meant for you.

And maybe you don't know what's next.
Maybe you don't even want to know.

But you know this:
You're not who you were.
And that's already a beginning.

Because maybe — just maybe —
you don't belong where you've been
because you're meant to build the place you're going.

And in this soft space between no and yes —
you're not waiting.
You're becoming.

P.S: If life feels like a bad party — it's okay to leave, even if you brought the snacks.

"What If I Mess Up" Syndrome

You know the moment. That microscopic moment where you think: "Should I do this?"

And before your soul can whisper "Yes," your brain grabs a dhol, calls your anxiety relatives, and throws a full shaadi — complete with baraat, buffet, and dramatic slow-mo crying — all for a wedding between *you* and *a hypothetical failure*.

Suddenly, it's 3:17 AM and you're wide awake, sweating about a career you haven't started, a mistake you haven't made, and a breakdown that hasn't even RSVP'd yet.

Because why wait for life to screw you over when you can self-destruct in advance, right?

You tell people you're "just being cautious." No, beta. You're mentally doomscrolling your own future. It's like your inner voice got drunk and turned into an astrologer who only predicts worst-case scenarios.

Meanwhile, you're paralyzed. Not because you're lazy — oh no — you're just *busy hallucinating failure*. In 4K. With subtitles.

But sure. Let's open a new tab and Google "How to start over when you haven't even started."

Trying Without Trying

So instead of doing the one terrifying thing that actually matters — you open five tabs, make chai, deep-clean the bathroom, and suddenly decide now is the right time to "research your life purpose" via a three-hour podcast hosted by a guy named Yash who lives in Goa and thinks hustle culture is a government conspiracy.

Because *doing something* — anything — gives you the illusion of progress. And illusions are way easier to handle than effort.

You call it prep. You romanticize it. But really, you're just emotionally outsourcing the fear of starting. You're performing productivity the way some people perform marriages — with lots of rituals, very little joy, and a nagging sense of "this wasn't the plan."

You stare at the blinking cursor. The unfinished email. The unsent form. But instead of typing, you re-watch that reel of a 9-year-old CEO who just launched a startup for biodegradable sketch pens. Meanwhile, your greatest achievement today was finally charging your power bank.

And no, it's not because you're lazy. It's because your brain is busy juggling 19 worst-case scenarios while your hands fold laundry like your career depends on it. Because laundry is safe. Laundry doesn't judge.

And in your head, you're negotiating with your own ambition: *"Give me two more days, yaar, I swear I'll start. Just… after this last YouTube rabbit hole."*

But it never ends. Because in 'What If' Land, doing anything real feels riskier than doing nothing at all.

You'll scrub your fridge, reply to old WhatsApp messages, clean your Gmail spam folder, and even rewatch *Taare Zameen Par* for "inspiration" — but you **will** not start that one real thing that might actually change your life.

Nobody Died from an Awkward Presentation — Except in My Head

There was this one time I genuinely thought I'd explode from shame during a class presentation. Not metaphorically. Like, actual *spontaneous combustion* from sheer social anxiety. All I had to do was talk. About a topic I *chose*. In front of people I'd eaten canteen samosas with.

And yet, there I was — sweating like I'd been dropped into a pressure cooker, hands trembling like a freshly born deer, and *somehow* pronouncing "entrepreneur". Three times.

But nobody threw tomatoes. No one stormed out yelling, *"This fraud must be stopped!"* People clapped. Some even smiled. And later, someone told me I was "relatable," which is a polite way of saying, "You looked like a mess, but a lovable one."

That's when it hit me — **maybe the shame wasn't real. Maybe it was just a story I told myself to justify staying small.**

Because let's be honest: we all think the world is watching us trip. When in reality, everyone's too busy rehearsing their own disasters. It's called the **spotlight effect** — where you assume people are noticing your every misstep, when in reality, they're probably just wondering if anyone noticed theirs.

You didn't bomb. You humaned.

And that? That's already impressive.

Because—If Babies Thought Like Adults, None of Us Would Be Walking

Imagine if babies had your overthinking adult brain. *"Hmm, what if I stand and fall? What if people laugh? What if I never walk perfectly and someone posts it on Instagram with the caption 'LMAO #FlopShow'?"*

That baby would still be crawling. In a three-piece suit. Late to work. Blaming Mercury retrograde.

But babies don't think like that. They fall. They cry. They stand again. And weirdly? No one tells them, *"You should've had a solid walking plan before attempting this."* Everyone just cheers and goes, *"Awww, look at him try!"*

So here's a question: when did *trying* become embarrassing?

When did stumbling stop meaning progress and start meaning shame?

Because if you only want to show up when you're perfect — congrats, you'll never show up.

Your brain learns by screwing up. That's how neuroplasticity works. Trial. Error. Learn. Repeat. That's how babies master walking. And it's also how adults master not ruining their own damn lives.

So get up. Wobble. Fall. Cry a little if you must. Then get your adult diapered ego up and try again.

And if anyone judges you for trying? Congrats — you've just found someone who's probably still crawling.

Fear Is Just Your Brain's Clingy Autocorrect — Hit 'Ignore' and Do It Anyway

Every time you try to do something remotely meaningful — like apply for that job, send that risky-but-honest message, pitch your weird-but-genius idea — your brain crashes the party like a clingy aunt who thinks you'll die if you wear ripped jeans.

"Beta, what if you fail? What if people laugh? What if you ruin your life, end up jobless, loveless, and eating Maggi in your childhood bedroom at 35?"

Relax. You're just starting a project, not stealing from the mafia.

Your brain is dramatic. It's the same part of you that thought your life was over when you mistakenly called your teacher "mom" in 6th grade. Or when you waved back at someone who wasn't actually waving at you. Or when you sneezed so loud in your college presentation that even the professor flinched.

You survived all that. And no one remembers. Except you — on loop — at 2 a.m. when you should be sleeping.

Here's the truth: **Your brain doesn't want you to thrive. It wants you to stay safe. And safety, unfortunately, is often just a fancy word for staying stuck.**

Your brain was designed for survival, not self-fulfillment. That voice in your head screaming *"DON'T DO IT"* is just a habit — not holy wisdom.

So yeah. You're scared. Good. Do it anyway. Hit "send." Say "yes." Fumble through it. Stammer. Sweat. Mess up the pronunciation of "entrepreneur" again.

Worst case? You fail and learn.

Best case? You win and grow.

Either way, it's better than color-coding your Google Drive folders and calling it progress.

And no, literally no one cares as much as you think they do. They're too busy overthinking their own awkward fart cum sneeze-in-public moment.

So click "ignore," Human. Growth doesn't wait for your anxiety to give permission.

Home Isn't Always Restful

Home is supposed to be your safe space, right? A place to recharge, be your messy self, that sacred space where you take off your Formals, wear that torn t-shirt from 2015, scratch your stomach, let out a loud fart, and finally feel safe enough to cry without having to explain why or in brief, existentially rot in peace.
Yeah, well, not if you're Indian.

Rest in an Indian household is like having relatives who mind their own business —sounds magical, but doesn't exist.

You walk in expecting calm, and boom—your dad's yelling because the AC remote has vanished (again), your mom's yelling because you're not married (again), and your sibling just used your charger, your towel, and probably your will to live, and the TV is playing a serial on full blast where a woman is being slapped in slow motion for the 83rd time.

And God forbid you try to take a nap. You could be dying. Actually dying. But if you dare lie down at 3 PM in an Indian household, suddenly you're not tired, you're *"lazy." You haven't even shut your eyes and suddenly there's a panel discussion happening around you — led by your mom, co-hosted by your Massi in the phone call.*

"Aaram? Din ke beech mein? Yeh hai tumhaari progress?"

It's no longer a nap. it's a lifestyle failure.

Because in Indian homes, rest is not recovery. Rest is rebellion. And naps? Naps are practically anti-national.

And just when you fake-sleep a little too convincingly, the housemaid knocks with chai she wanted for herself but *conveniently* made "for you"— her own eyes screaming *"I needed this more, but okay, let the privileged one sip first."*

Love Served Passive-Aggressively

You ever try leaving the house for a trip without causing an emotional earthquake?

No matter how nicely you dress, how early you finish your chores, how politely you say, "Main bas 2 din mein aa jaunga," the moment your hand touches the door handle, your mom is already halfway into a tragic monologue about how she sacrificed her dreams so you could party in ripped jeans and chill with "BODMAS DOSTS"

It's not a trip anymore—it's a guilt trip wrapped in turmeric and tears, and hidden 500 note in your back pack with one Goodday biscuit packet.

See, in Indian home, **love shows up loud and late.**

They don't say "I love you," but they'll remember how you like your Maggi—with extra masala and no peas.

They won't ask how your day was, but they'll notice the silence in your voice and make your favorite chai, pretending it's for themselves.

You're told not to cry because "you have to be strong." But the minute you hold it in too well, you're labeled cold.
You're encouraged to rest, but not too much. Rest quickly becomes laziness. "Be useful" becomes the background music to every Sunday nap attempt.
And when someone asks what's wrong, they don't want the real answer. They want *nothing, just tired*. Safe answer. Digestible answer. End of conversation.

In our homes, love isn't usually direct. It's not, "I love you, I'm proud of you."
It's more like… "Have some food."
It's your dad giving you extra money while you are going out.
It's your mom calling to ask if you had lunch but sneaking in a "don't waste money on Zomato" mid-call.
It's your sibling sending you a meme after a fight, like a peace offering wrapped in sarcasm.

This is how we've all grown up—surrounded by unspoken affection wrapped in instructions and judgment and strangely timed concern.
You know they mean well. You do. But sometimes, their version of love feels like walking barefoot on broken glass. You understand the intention, but it still cuts.

And it's exhausting.

Because you're constantly decoding what's being said vs. what's being felt.
You're managing your emotions while buffering theirs.
You become the responsible one. The "sorted" one. The one who handles things.
Who doesn't cause trouble. Who keeps the peace.

And quietly, that peace turns into pressure.

You can't fall apart, because if you do, who's going to hold it together?
So you don't rest. Not really. Not even at home. Especially not at home.

Because sometimes, home isn't where you recover.
It's where you rehearse your strength.

Sorted Outside, Scrambled Inside.

You weren't the dramatic one. You were the Wi-Fi password knower, the water bottle filler, the one who reminded mom to take her blood pressure medicine and dad to take his blood sugar seriously. You were the family's unpaid life manager before you even had leg hair.

No tantrums, no rebellion—just strategic silence and the ability to guess when someone was about to blow up over a misplaced TV remote.

You were the *sorted one.*

Not because your life was sorted—but because your breakdowns were politely postponed till everyone else's were handled.

You were the soft landing for everyone else's breakdowns.
The peacemaker. The fixer. The one who knew when to change the topic, when to make chai.

You were a child whose emotional adulthood arrived way too early — trying to balance the volume of your father's silence, your mother's tears, your sibling's tantrum, and your own report card.

And then, one day, you leave home. But only physically. Sort of. Moved out.
Sort of.
Because you never really leave the house you were emotionally raised in.

The real home — the one that shaped your nervous system — it packs itself into your suitcase.
Quietly. Like guilt. Like expectation. Like a playlist you didn't ask for but keeps auto-playing in the background.

You enter new spaces — colleges, jobs, relationships — and something always feels... unfamiliar.

Someone says, *"Take your time."*
You panic. Because what's the catch? No one gives time for free where you come from.

Someone asks, *"What do you need right now?"*
And your brain freezes. You've never been asked that. At home, needs weren't something you voiced. They were something you adjusted.

You flinch at comfort. You're suspicious of soft love.
You confuse calm with distance.
You mistake criticism as care — because that's how it was served to you.

And now? You overthink texts.
You apologize for having boundaries.
You try to be chill about things that are actually hurting.
Because your inner home still tells you:
"Too much emotion makes people uncomfortable. Too much need makes you selfish."

So you micromanage your feelings like unpaid overtime.
You host people in your life while evicting your own comfort.
You talk yourself out of crying, out of resting, out of asking for things — because at some point, you learned that being okay was the most convenient version of you.

And you wonder why peace feels so damn unfamiliar.

The truth?
You were just trying to keep the house from falling apart.
But now, you're the one carrying all the broken pieces — inside your chest, inside your choices, inside your relationships.

You didn't want to be strong. You just didn't have a choice.

And now strength is your reflex. Even when you're tired. Even when you're loved. Even when no one's asking you to be.

BUT, WAIT,

Whom are we blaming?

Maybe they weren't bad at loving you—maybe they were just busy surviving themselves.

Everyone's First Time at This

You spent years trying to decode their silence, thinking love was something you had to earn by being less of a burden.

Sometimes, the people who were supposed to protect your peace were too busy battling their own storms to notice they became your chaos.

Your dad? Probably never said "I love you." But you still remember how he'd silently leave the last piece of mango for you, as if that made up for all the conversations that never happened. Your mom won't sit down for five minutes but will yell from the kitchen about how nobody loves her—while also refilling your plate with food she swears she's too tired to make. Your sibling? They act like they don't care, but they always know when your favorite show's on, or when you're quieter than usual—and they'll pass you the remote without saying much.

And you? You became the fixer. The one who made the jokes at dinner, who diffused the tension when tempers rose. You learned too young how to read moods like warning signs. You learned how to tiptoe through conversations. You learned that sometimes, peace means silence—even if that silence is slowly rotting you from the inside.

And yet, here's the kicker: no one here is the villain. Not your father who shut down. Not your mother who weaponized her pain. Because maybe your dad never learned how to talk about emotions. Maybe your mom was raised to believe rest is selfish.

And Your sibling? Might be sitting ten feet away from you, yet you've never really known what's on their mind. You assume they're fine because they're not crying. But the truth is, they've been drowning quietly in an ocean of unspoken things. And you didn't ask because you were barely keeping your own head above water.

Nobody in your house meant to hurt you. They were just trying to survive— just like you. They were just people. Still figuring it out. Still learning how to be parents, children, partners, siblings—while life threw bills, betrayal, and back pain at them like a badly written soap opera.

But that doesn't mean it didn't hurt.
That doesn't mean it was okay.
That doesn't mean you didn't deserve better.

It just means—
maybe everyone was doing their best with what they had...
Kind of Survival Love?

But survival love is noisy. It comes wrapped in guilt, in mood swings, in backhanded compliments, in taunts that hit just a little too hard. It shows up as cutting fruits without asking, or waiting for you to get home before eating, or silently taking your side in front of a screaming relative.

They may never say "I'm proud of you," or "I'm sorry," or even "I love you." But they'll charge your phone. They'll wait up at night when you're late. They'll pass you a blanket when you fall asleep on the sofa.

And while that's love... it's also a lot to carry.

Because when you grow up around love that whispers instead of speaks, that reacts instead of reflects, you start second-guessing every version of love the world offers you. You start believing it's your job to translate everyone's silence into meaning—and that becomes exhausting.

Sometimes you get it right.
Sometimes you get hurt.
Sometimes you hurt others.

And I again repeat no one's the villain here. Not your dad who shuts down. Not your mom who loses it over small things. Not your sibling who's always in their room. Not even you, for being tired of holding it all together.

Everyone's just showing up to life with no manual, pretending they're the expert.

So if it feels messy, it's because it is.
If it feels unfair, it probably is.
But maybe, just maybe... it's everyone's first time at this.

Rebuilding the Nest (Even If You Start Alone)

You don't heal a house by yelling at the walls.

You heal it by becoming the room you wish existed.

The kind of room where people are allowed to feel things without being labelled "too emotional."
Where silence doesn't mean distance.

Where a mistake isn't met with drama, but with a simple, "Okay, let's figure it out."

You heal it by talking—even if your voice trembles, even if the words feel clumsy in your mouth, even if nobody knows what to say back.
Because the truth is, no one taught our parents emotional vocabulary.
No one taught us either.

We were all just... surviving. Cracking jokes. Taking jabs. Passing plates. Saving face.
And somewhere between, love got lost in the noise.

But that doesn't mean you have to carry the pain with you forever.
You're allowed to put it down.

You're allowed to build something softer—first inside you, and then around you.
You don't need to become the family therapist.
You just need to become the person **you** would've run to as a child.

Start there.

Be the one who doesn't mock tears.
Who says, "Tell me more," instead of "Tu overthink karta hai."
Who understands that sometimes, the loudest people are the ones most afraid to be alone with themselves.

Maybe your home won't change overnight. Maybe your dad will still change the channel when things get too emotional. Maybe your mom will still guilt-trip you with food and unfinished phone calls.
But maybe, one day, they'll knock on your door—not to scold you, but to sit next to you. Quietly. Curiously. Comfortably.

Because you didn't just rebuild a nest.
You **became** it.

And in doing so, you taught the whole house what rest could feel like.

Even if it started with you, alone.

"Maybe healing your home doesn't start with them understanding you—maybe it starts with you forgiving the silence they didn't know how to fill."

Never With Dad

In every Indian house, there's a silent, unsaid agreement:
You talk to Mom. She talks to Dad.
And you pretend that's not what's happening.

You could break your phone, your heart, your career plans — and you'd still go to
Mom first. Not because she's softer. But because she's the filter.
Dad? Indian kids don't take such risks.

So you go to Mom at 11 PM:
"Listen, don't tell Dad. Please."
She nods. She gets it. She acts so scared you feel like even God wouldn't dare to
let the secret out.

Then next morning, Dad's reading the newspaper and casually drops:
"So… what's this new plan of quitting your job to become a food blogger?"

And that's when it hits you.
Mom didn't tell him. She **leaked** it.
Through *looks*, *sighs*, and that one perfectly timed "I was just saying…" while
making tea.

And weirdly, we never confronted it.
We just swallowed the fact that he knows.
Because his silence wasn't ignorance — it was a choice.
He heard. He processed. He moved on.
No lectures. No drama. Just… a slightly louder cough during dinner.

And somewhere between these cold-war-style conversations,
you started holding back.
Started editing parts of yourself before even thinking them.
Not because he didn't care.
But because you never learned **how** to say it.

Because dads in our homes aren't raised to ask,
"What's going on in your head?"
And we aren't raised to answer, **"Everything."**

So we made this little pact with ourselves —
"Tell him only when it's good news. Or necessary. Or after Mom softens the landing."

And that's how we became strangers who live in the same house and ask about cricket scores more than real feelings.

Because it was always safer to say:
"Tell Mom, she'll tell him."

Even if we knew —
She already has.

Filtered Feelings

You never really *told* Dad things.
They just… reached him.

Through Mom.
Through silence.
Through the long sighs after your door slammed shut.

You'd confess something to your mother — heartbreak, anxiety, the kind of existential crisis that starts with "What even is the point?"
And somewhere between her nodding and her comforting,
your secret got repackaged with: *Extras.*

Next morning, Dad behaves… differently.
A little too normal.
The tea already poured, the newspaper already folded, your favourite side of the omelette facing you.
As if *that* could patch up whatever was broken inside.

He won't ask.
But he *knows*.
And that strange silence — It's effort.
The kind he was never trained to show.

Because he didn't grow up with emotional vocabulary.

He grew up with quiet rooms and loud responsibilities.
His father didn't ask him how he felt.
His mother didn't either.
So he learned to love… by showing up, not by speaking up.

So now, *you* want words.
But all he has is presence.

And it hurts.
Not because he doesn't care —
but because he doesn't know **how** to show that he does.

And maybe that's where it all breaks —
between the *what you needed*,
and the *only way he knew how to give*.

Because love in Indian households is different.
It's not I-love-you texts or heartfelt hugs.
It's asking if you've eaten.
It's checking the tyre pressure of your scooty.
It's silently Googling your symptoms after you say you're "just tired."

It's real. It's deep.
But it's **rarely spoken.**

Polite Distances

You don't remember the exact day it started — maybe when you flinched before speaking. Maybe when you watched your dad reading the newspaper, and realised some pages would never fold open between the two of you.

It wasn't war. It wasn't cold either. It was just… polite.

Conversations became task lists.
"Did you eat?"
"Did you pay the bill?"
"Tell your mother."

And slowly, between these logistical check-ins, you unlearned vulnerability.
You stopped saying what hurt.
He stopped asking what mattered.

You never hated him. You just stopped bothering him with your truths.
And he — maybe out of habit, or maybe fear — never knocked twice.

You're dying to talk. He's dying to care.
But you're both stuck in this deeply uncomfortable politeness..

And maybe it's not their fault.
Maybe your mom was raised to protect,
and your dad was raised to perform.

She was taught emotions are private.
He was taught emotions are weakness.

So when you cried into your pillow,
your dad knew — but said nothing.
When you failed, he felt it — but blinked through it.
And when you wanted a hug, you asked Mom instead.
Because that's how it was done.
That's how it's *always* been done.

Inherited Silences

You didn't wake up one day and decide to stop sharing things with your dad.
You just… slowly stopped.
Like how an old fan loses speed — not because it's broken, but because it's tired.

And if you're being honest,
maybe you didn't start the silence.
Maybe you just picked it up from him.

You saw him go through things without ever naming them.
Watched him power through work stress, family loss, bills, health scares —
like they were just… things to get done. No breakdowns. No sighs. Just a quiet
nod and another task ticked off the list.

He never told you he was hurting.
So when it was your turn to hurt — you thought silence was the language for it.

He never cried in front of his father.
Now you can't imagine crying in front of him.

It wasn't about pride. Or ego.
It was just how things were.

That's how he was with his dad.
And now... that's how you are with him.

You both sit in the same room sometimes,
scrolling on phones, sipping tea,
thinking of the ten things you *could* say —
but instead, settling for:
"Will Modi become the next PM?"

And in that silence, there's not anger.
There's a strange kind of love. But also... a grief.
For everything that could've been shared, but never was.

You start to realise —
this isn't just *your* emotional wiring.
It's inheritance.
Passed down not through genetics...
but through glances, nods, and the things we never found the words for.

And that?
That hurts in a way that's hard to describe.
Because he didn't fail you.
You didn't fail him.
But the gap is still there.
And neither of you knows who's supposed to build the bridge.

Quiet Repairs

Maybe it's time we realise...
he's human too.
He wasn't born a father. He became one the day we showed up.
And from that moment on, he's been figuring it out. Quietly. On his own.
Like we've been trying to figure ourselves out — just with fewer tools and a lot
more responsibility.

Maybe he needs a friend. Not one who expects him to have all the answers,
but someone who's willing to sit down and ask,
"How are you really doing, Dad?"

It's strange.
We'd never want our own child to cry alone, to hide their feelings from us.
But somehow, we grew up doing just that with him.

And maybe it wasn't about love.
Maybe it was about fear.
Or timing. Or generation gaps. Or just… habit.

And maybe — just maybe —
he wasn't cold. He was just scared of saying the wrong thing.
He didn't know how to show it.
So he packed your bags for school.
Made your sandwich without asking.
Stood outside the doctor's office pacing, while Mom held your hand inside.

We spent years waiting for big words. For open arms. For warmth in a language
we understood.
But maybe his version of love didn't come in words.
Maybe it came in quiet routines, and sacrifices we were too young to notice.

And now?
Now we're older.
And we can reach too.

It doesn't need a big apology or a deep conversation.
Sometimes it just needs a seat next to him on the sofa.
Two cups of chai. A question about his day.
A little more curiosity. A little less pride.

Because the relationship you wanted?
It might still be waiting.
Not in the past — but right here, quietly hoping someone would go first.

And if one day, your kid asks you —
"What kind of father is your dad?"

Maybe you'll say,
"A little distant, but always there.
Not perfect… but we found our way back to each other.
Slowly.

And then maybe — just maybe —
you'll sit a little closer to your own child.
So they never have to wait that long to ask.
Or to know.

Too Close to Heal From

We've all had *that* one person.
The one you'd drop everything for.
No explanation needed, no questions asked — just one call and you'd show up.
That *one person* in your life you would do literally anything for?
Yeah. This chapter is about *that* person.
The one you'd cancel plans, share fries, give your Netflix password, kidney… whatever.

They were your emergency contact.
Hell, they were your *everything contact*. Not love. Not even friendship, technically.
But whatever it was, it felt… sacred.

And then one fine day — boom.
They ghost you. Block you. Move on.

You?
You're left standing there.

And here's the best part — there wasn't even a breakup.
Because apparently, if it's not a relationship, it can't officially *end*.
It just… fades. Like that New Year's resolution…

No warning, no season finale — they disappeared.
No "we need to talk."
Just a digital vanishing act.
Blocked, archived, demoted from "Favourite chat" to "Do not disturb."
You're still here, pretending it doesn't hurt, forwarding memes to them on impulse, and realising they don't even follow you anymore.
Still low-key stalking their Spotify to see if they've moved on to sad ghazals or "healing playlist vol. 4."
Still watching their stories from a fake account, pretending it's not you behind the profile of "Angel _Priya 420."
Still telling your friends,
"No, no, they're not a bad person. Just… complicated."

Still Here, Still Hurting.

You don't bring them up anymore.
Not because you're over it — but because the people around you *are*.

You still check your phone sometimes — not because you're expecting a text, but because some part of your muscle memory still belongs to them.

They didn't block you.
You didn't unfollow.
You just learned to stop reacting when their name popped up in someone else's story.

There's no soundtrack to this kind of heartbreak.
No violins. No 'Bada Pachtaoge'.
Just a casual silence that feels more humiliating than hate.

And the worst part?
You're still the keeper of their secrets.
Still defending them in your head.
Still rewriting history so they look a little less cruel.

You once told them things you hadn't even told yourself.
And now you flinch when someone asks, "Are you okay?"
Because how do you explain grief for someone who technically didn't leave — they just stopped arriving?

Some nights, you catch yourself drafting a message.
Not to rekindle anything. Just… to remind them you existed.
Then you delete it. Not out of pride, but because you're scared they won't reply.

And that — that's the part that hurts more than anything they ever did.

Not the silence.
Not the distance.
But the fact that you kept choosing them in rooms where they never even looked back.

You want to scream. But you don't.
You just sigh.
Take a longer shower.
And carry on — like the grown-up everyone expects you to be.

No tears.
Just the quiet ache of knowing someone saw your insides and still chose to look away.

Quiet Quit

You don't stalk anymore.
Not because you healed — but because there's nothing left to refresh. You just ran out of things to look at.
Your curiosity lost patience.
And your self-respect finally said, *"Bro, this is embarrassing now."*

You scroll past their name like it's any other piece of data.
Your thumb doesn't pause.
Your heart doesn't glitch.
And that silence?
It's not forgiveness.
Is it? May be. May be NOT.

You stop asking *why it ended*.
Because let's be honest — if it had a name, it could've been fixed.
But it didn't.
No breakup. No closure. Just quiet exits and messy assumptions.

So you start asking different questions.
Not *why did they leave?*
But *why the hell did I shrink so small just to make space for them?*

And no — you don't miss *them*.
You miss *you*…
The version of you that still believed.
That still called first.
That still thought loyalty was… Nevermind

Now?
You're not looking for new people.
You're just trying to become someone *you* don't abandon in the process.

And that's the hard part —
Learning to show up for yourself,
even when they didn't.

Forgiveness is weird

It's not an event — it's a practice. Like brushing your teeth. Or ignoring their birthday every year on purpose.

You don't wake up one morning with glitter in your chest saying,
"I forgive them."
No. You just stop checking if they watched your story.

You stop rehearsing the argument you'll never get to have.
You stop proving you were the better one.
You stop needing them to know they hurt you.

Because by now, you do know this:
Forgiveness isn't for them. It's to free yourself from carrying their mess like it was yours.

You're not excusing what they did.
You're just… done renting space in your mind to someone who didn't even pay attention.

And as for forgetting?

Well… let's not rush it.

Maybe, if you're lucky, you'll forget the details.
But not the lesson. Never the lesson.

The Exit

You don't get closure.
You get clarity — in painfully honest pieces.
Not all at once, and definitely not when you want it.

There's no dramatic last scene.
No final text that explains everything.
No background score swelling as they realise what they lost.
Just… silence.
And a version of you that's finally done rehearsing forgiveness for someone who never asked for it.

Eventually, you realise:
Some people leave in a way that teaches you how to stay — with yourself.

You don't hate them anymore.
You just don't glorify them either.
You stop rewriting history to make sense of their absence.

That love? That trust? That blind, bleeding devotion?
You're reclaiming it.
Not to lock it away —
But to give wisely. Deliberately. Only to those who know what it's worth.

Because the real healing?
It's not about becoming colder.
It's about staying soft — but with better boundaries.
Not bitter, just better.

And now, you're not afraid to walk away either.
Not to punish them.
But to protect *you.*

Because we only live once.
And what a tragedy it would be —
to spend that one, wild, irreplaceable life
waiting for love in a place that makes you feel
homeless in your own heart.

Give your time to someone who shows up.
Maybe a friend. A sibling. A stranger who became family.
Anyone —
but not the one who made your love feel like a burden. Not the one who taught
you how to beg for crumbs
in a feast you helped build. This world is actually starving for the love you have
been pouring in the underserved's cup.

Because healing isn't forgetting.
It's remembering who you are —
and choosing not to disappear for anyone ever again.

So if you're looking for a sign to stop breaking your own heart for someone who
never deserved your softness — this is it.

Let this be the day you stop bleeding for people who wouldn't even notice your
bandages.
Let this be the chapter you write for *you.*

Even My Pain Has to Be Manly

No one ever said it out loud, but somewhere along the way, every man learns this one rule — if it hurts, bury it. If you cry, hide it. And if you break... do it quietly.

They never give you a "how-to" guide for being a man.
But there's an unspoken syllabus:
Don't cry. Don't complain. Don't be weak.
Be reliable. Be the rock. Be the guy who doesn't flinch — even when it's burning inside.

So you learn to wear your wounds like badges.
Smiling while your heart cramps in silence.
Laughing during pain because that's what strong men do — right? Crack a joke.
Flex a little. Die a little inside.

You become fluent in the art of saying "I'm good"
When you're anything but.

And when someone asks, "What's up?"
You respond with Kohli's scores.
Not the fact that your chest's been feeling like it's holding back a storm for three months straight.

Because you've been taught that being a man means being invincible.
Which is just a cooler way of saying — no one's coming to check if you're okay.

And the worst part?
You start believing that you don't deserve a shoulder. That the only time you're allowed to fall apart
is **never**.

Alone, Among Brothers

There's always a group. The gang. The boys.

You're not really alone.
The boys are always around.
Someone's sending reels, someone's cribbing about traffic, someone's planning a
Goa trip .. Russians.. (coughs)

But no one's really asking: "How are you?"
Because boys don't do that.
They ask, "Beer?" and hope you'll say everything after one bottle.

And maybe you try.
You crack a joke about not sleeping, drop a half-sentence about feeling off.
Someone laughs. Someone says it's common. Someone say's it's nothing.
You move on.

Because if you say more, they'll get uncomfortable.
And if they say more, you'll get scared.

It's not their fault. They're just like you.
Grew up hearing: "Real men handle it."
"Strong boys don't cry."
"Be a man. Walk it off."

So now?
You can say you're broke.
You can say your boss sucks.
You can even joke about dying alone.

But you can't say:
"I'm scared."
"I feel like I'm failing."
"I don't know how to keep going."

Because that's not "cool."
That's "awkward."

And maybe the loneliest you've ever felt...
wasn't in a breakup.
Or when a friend stopped calling.
But in a room full of your own brothers.

Your childhood best friends.
The group chat guys.
Your cousins.
Even the ones who check in on your mom when you're away.

You all sit, shoulder to shoulder.
Sharing snacks. Trading jokes.
Scrolling past memes.
Not one word about what really hurts.

Because in between the laughter and leg-pulling,
there's a silence no one's willing to disturb.
A fear that the moment you say something real,
the room will shift.
The dynamic will change.
You'll be the one who made it "awkward."

So you speak less.
Feel more.
And convince yourself that you're the only one who feels this invisible distance.

But here's the twist nobody admits—
They feel it too.
Your brother. Your best friend. The guy who always seems "sorted."

You all miss each other... silently.
You all love each other... poorly.

Because no one ever taught you how to say,
"Hey, I'm hurting too."
So you throw another joke in the air,
and hope it catches what you couldn't say.

Manly Silence?

You could be shattered inside...
and still carry the gas cylinder up three floors.
Because who else will?

You could be grieving the loss of someone you never got to say goodbye to —
and still show up for your cousin's wedding and smile for 87 photos.
Because *"log kya kahenge"* if you don't?

There's no space —
not in your family WhatsApp,
not in your chai break conversations,
not even in your own reflection —
for saying:
"I'm not okay."

So you have to be-
Strong. Collected. Always in control.
And somehow, even your breakdowns... feel choreographed.
Postponed till the house is asleep.
Muted behind closed bathroom doors.
Brief, clean, quiet.

No mess. No drama. No tears on the shirt collar.
Because someone might notice.

Your Pain isn't forbidden.
It's just supposed to come dressed in a manly form.
Delivered with a steady voice.
Mentioned lightly, with a chuckle —
"Yeah, that time was tough, bro..."

You don't cry. You cope.
You don't vent. You function.
And the world claps for your "strength,"
unaware that it's killing you silently.

Somewhere along the line,
survival became your habit.
Grief turned into a daily commute.
Anxiety became background noise.

You didn't stop feeling.
You just stopped showing.

And now?
You lift the weight of your world
Because nobody taught you
how to drop it without being called weak.

Permission to Feel

You're not crying in the rain.
You're crying in the bathroom. At your cousin's wedding. While everyone else is doing the hook step to "Ghungroo."

And it's not even about the wedding. It's the email you got that morning. The job rejection. The memory of someone you used to talk to every night. The way your dad still doesn't say "I'm proud of you" even when you've done everything right.

It's everything — all at once — coming undone while you stare at a Jaquar tap wondering how much water one person can waste before someone knocks.

This is the Indian adult man's first real breakdown.
Not poetic. Just quietly tragic.

There's no therapist couch in sight. No friend with whiskey and tissues.
Just you... and the mirror in your childhood bedroom, where the stickers from your Class 4 Science Project are still half hanging.

You look into that mirror — and suddenly, the mask you've been wearing starts to feel *too tight.*

All your life, you were told: *"Don't cry, be strong."*
But no one told you that strength doesn't mean silence.
No one told you that the wall you became... was also the wall you crashed into.

Because the truth is — the first time you *really* let go, it won't be beautiful.
It'll be weird. Awkward. You'll cry and then apologise to *yourself* for being "dramatic."
But it'll also be real.

And real?
That's rare.

Sometimes it starts small.
A friend doesn't laugh off your sadness.
A colleague says, "Take care of yourself," and actually *means* it.
Your mom says, "You're working too much," and you don't argue this time.

And just like that... you start feeling.
Not just thinking.
Not just functioning.

Feeling.

The bills still need to be paid.
The water purifier still needs servicing.
Your boss still wants that file before 5pm.

But something inside you… unclenches.. or in simple terms.. relaxes
Not because everything is solved.
But because you finally gave yourself permission to admit:
"I'm not okay. But I want to be."

And for a man who's always been the punchline, the provider, the pillar —
that single moment of softness?

That's the start of healing.. sorry.. LIVING.

Redefining Strength

What if strength was never about how much you can lift…
but how much you can let go?

What if the strongest thing a man could do
was *not* suppress it, swallow it, bury it —
but to *feel it*, face it, and *still* stand up the next morning and make tea for his mother?

Maybe that's strength too.
You've lived your whole life being the backup charger.
The one who's supposed to hold it together,
Fix the bulb. Fill the petrol. Hide the panic attack.
Send money home. And never send your own pain to anyone else's inbox.

But here's what no one told you:

You're not just a man.
You're a *human*.
And humans break. But they also rebuild.

So now —
Don't just carry the weight.
Question it.
Who told you that being soft meant being small?

That crying made you 'girlish'?

That rest was weakness?

Who said masculinity meant doing everything *alone*?

You were never built to be a rock.

You were born a river —
meant to move, meant to flood, meant to crash and *still* find your way.

Let your strength be *kind* now.
Let it have roots *and* wings.

Because maybe... strength is also:
- Asking for help before your body gives out.
- Saying "no" without guilt.
- Loving deeply, without needing to rescue.
- Telling your son he's allowed to cry.
- Telling your father he's allowed to try again.
- Being the first man in your family who breaks the cycle — not bones.

The world taught you how to endure like a man.
Now teach it how to heal like one too.

Not by bleeding in silence.
But by *choosing* to live. Loudly. Softly. Honestly. Crying because you miss someone, or loving with teary eyes, doesn't make you any less of a man — it just means you had the guts to feel what most run from.

She's a Bro

A girl who didn't pick sides — so society picked one for her.

She never asked to be different.
She just didn't like being told who she was supposed to be.

She wasn't a cricketer.
She wasn't a mechanic.
She was just a girl who didn't like what she was *supposed* to like — and that was enough for the world to lose its mind.

In the **kids' playroom,** she picked the red car instead of the pink kitchen set.
No one said much. But their eyebrows did.

In the **living room**, she beat her cousin in arm wrestling.
Everyone laughed. Called her strong.
Then added, *"You'll scare boys away."*
Like her strength was something to tone down for someone else's comfort.

In the **school corridor**, she walked like she owned the place.
Boys high-fived her.
Girls looked confused.
Teachers said she was "too loud,"
like girlhood only came in a whisper.

In the **drawing room**, relatives pointed at her short hair and asked,
"That's your son, right?"
Someone replied,
"No, no — that's our daughter."

She wasn't trying to be a tomboy. She was just… being efficient. Why wear a frock that flies while running, when track pants have pockets *and* dignity?

She wasn't loud.
She was just honest.
And that's a problem if you're a girl in India —
because sugarcoating is considered *sanskari*.

She didn't sit like a lady.
She sat like someone who wanted to be comfortable.
And in Indian houses, comfort has gender restrictions.

At birthday parties, while other girls were getting mehendi, she was asking the caterer about how they fit 400 samosas in one steel drum.

But in a society where femininity comes with a manual —
when you skip a few chapters, they write a new category for you:

Tomboy.

Like it's a phase.
A glitch.
A rebellion.

Not just... a girl who doesn't like Pink.

Bhai.. Bro.. or something like that

Other girls walked into Class 8 looking like they had just stepped out of a *Clean & Clear* ad.

They suddenly started carrying pouches.
You carried your tiffin.

They dabbed compact powder before assembly.
You dabbed sweat off your forehead with your jersey sleeve.

You still thought lip balm was a winter thing, not a fashion statement.
One girl said, "It's tinted."
You genuinely asked, "Is that... a disease?"

At recess, the girls ate *less* — just so they could rush to the washroom and have their five-minute "touch-up" time.
You?

You finished your dabba.
And then half of Neha's paratha when she said she was "dieting."

You were too busy racing boys in the corridor to notice when your body started changing.
Until one day your mother said, "It's time we buy you... clothes from the women's section now."

Women's section?
The only thing you had in common with the mannequins was that both of you stood awkwardly in public spaces.

But amidst all this... there was *him*.

That boy.
The only boy who passed you the football with *style*.
Who high-fived you a little longer than others.
Who once said, "You're chill, ya."

You didn't call it a crush.

All you knew was you started brushing your hair before class and even borrowed your cousin's nice socks. (*The ones without holes.*)
You just… smiled when he entered the room.
Fixed your posture.
Tried not to look too eager when he sat next to you in Chemistry.

And then, one afternoon, out of nowhere — like it meant nothing, like *you* meant nothing , he Said —

"Bhai, pencil milega?"

Bhai.

BHAI ?

Not cute.
Not cool.
Not even neutral.
Just... *a moment*

The moment that rewired your DNA.
You didn't just lose a crush.
You lost your *gender* for 0.3 seconds.

And all you could do was hand over the pencil.
With the same hand you'd once imagined maybe, possibly, holding his.

Miss-Fit

You never asked to be different.
You just were. You've never really *fit*.
And for the longest time, that was okay. Like, *"Main alag hoon bhai. Ye sab mujhe suit nahi karta."*
But slowly, alag starts feeling… alone.

The boys? They love you.
You're the one who can lift 2 chairs together and doesn't cry in arguments.
You can carry a bike helmet and a friend's secret, equally well.
You're their bro.
Their wingman.
Their *launda with long hair.*

Until… they start talking about *"ladkiyaan."*
And you're suddenly reminded — *you are one.*

You're there, laughing, making jokes —
And then a sentence hits you sideways.
"She's hot, yaar. Not like those tomboy types."
And no one realises they just folded you in half, right there on the couch.

But you don't say anything.
You just laugh a little louder.
Because what else will you do? Ruin the vibe?

Once at a cousin's wedding, they asked you to help carry the crates because you looked "strong."
But didn't let you sit with the men during the whiskey round because "ladki ho, thoda tameez."

Then one day you're in the metro.
You're lost in thought, hoodie up, bag slung low.
Someone taps you from behind and says:

"Bhaiya, side de do."
And you're not even surprised.

Because, remember your crush?
He Called you "bro."
And you smiled.
Because reacting would've made it real.

And girls?
They bond over eyeshadow and breakups.
You try to join — but you've got no vocabulary for either.
They ask, "What shade do you use?"
You say, "Shade? Of what?"
And they laugh.
You laugh too.

But when you're alone that night,
You stare at the ceiling and think:
"If I'm not one of them, and not one of these... toh hoon kya main?"

PERIOD.

So... Is She a Tom Woman Now?

They used to say:

"Beta, girls don't sit like that."
"Girls don't talk like that."
"Girls don't fight, run, swear, dominate, argue."

And then years pass...

And suddenly, they clap for:

The boss lady who runs a team.
The CEO who doesn't flinch in a boardroom.
The biker woman with 1M Instagram followers.
The one who doesn't cry when her husband cheats, she *divorces* him and updates her LinkedIn.

The same traits.

The same woman.

The only difference? **Age. And success.**

As a kid, she was "too loud," "too wild," "too much of a boy."
Now? She's the TEDx speaker in your YouTube algorithm.

So let's ask the real question:
If a young girl who climbs trees and fixes punctures is a **tomboy**,
then when she grows up to negotiate salaries and fix broken homes —
is she a tom woman?

Or is she just your idea of a "strong woman"… with no credit for how she got
strong in the first place?

Because the truth is:

You didn't choose the tomboy…
Until she became useful to capitalism.

So tell us:

Was the problem that she was different?
Or that she didn't wait for your permission to be?

Because everything you now applaud —
her ambition, her grit, her "don't-need-a-man" energy —
were the very things you told her to "calm down" about in school.

So either clap for the tomboy *then*,
or admit you only love a strong woman **after she's earned your respect by
surviving your judgement.**

And maybe… just maybe…
instead of asking if she was "too boyish,"
you could've asked yourself:
Why are your definitions of a girl so damn small?

It Is What It is ..

She didn't "become" a tomboy.
She just didn't "become" the girl they expected.

She liked pockets.
She liked jumping off stairs.
She liked fixing the fan more than posing under it.

She wasn't trying to prove anything.
She wasn't "not like other girls."
She just happened to be exactly like herself — and apparently, that was a whole identity crisis for everyone else.

Let's get one thing straight:
She's not confused. **You are.**

You want your women to be strong, but gentle.
Loud, but only when it's cute.
Independent, but not intimidating.

And then comes a girl who doesn't care for the script.
She wears a jersey to a wedding, burps after the Pepsi, opens the car bonnet before calling her dad.
And now suddenly, you're uncomfortable?

She doesn't need your label.
She doesn't need a "phase."
She definitely doesn't need your advice on how to "balance it out."

Because while you were busy asking "Tomboy kyun hai?",
she already grew up, made her choices,
and figured out life is better when you don't waste it trying to fit into a dressing room that never had your size.

She wasn't a misfit — she just fit into places that didn't exist yet in Society's vocabulary.

Universe'S ON DND

———— ❖ ————

There's a special kind of heartbreak in realising the universe might be ignoring you on purpose.

Ever waited at a restaurant, dead hungry, with good food smells hijacking your sanity? The kind of hunger where even the paper napkin starts looking like a snack. You see the plates passing by — hot, fancy, Instagrammable — so tempting that for half a second, you seriously consider snatching that butter naan off the aunty's plate next to you.

Then it happens.
The kitchen door swings open

The waiter walks out.
With a plate.
Your plate. Obviously. It has to be yours.
Everyone else is already chewing. Who else is left?

He walks slowly. Carefully. Looks at you. Smiles.
And just when your taste buds start prepping for impact — You've swallowed so much saliva, your body's considering it the appetizer.

And then —
he **walks right past you** and serves it to the table behind.
Not even a glance back. No apology. No "your order is on the way."
Just pure betrayal on a steel plate.

That, my friend, is what manifesting feels like sometimes.

You ask. You wait. You believe. You even thank it in advance.
And in return? The universe serves your hopes to someone who didn't even ask for extra cheese.
You get ghosted by fate, left on "read" by destiny.

You're out here aligning chakras, scripting, 5-5-5 journaling…
The universe? Seen-zoned you. No typing bubble. No reply. Just ghosted by fate.
Meanwhile, someone got your damn pizza

The worst part?
You can't even complain.
Because every motivational guru is out here gaslighting you with "Divine Timing"
and at least three Instagram reels telling you:

"Raise your vibration."
"Maybe it wasn't meant for you."
Meanwhile, your manifestations are buffering on 2G while everyone else seems to
be on cosmic Wi-Fi.

This isn't just disappointment.
It's a slow-roasted, universe-certified heartbreak.
Served cold. With a side of "maybe it's not meant for you."

And yet?
You tip the damn waiter with gratitude anyway.
Because that's what we're taught — trust the timing, even if you're starving.

And maybe you do.
Because deep down, you still believe your order's coming.

Every time you say "things can't get worse," the universe takes it personally.

You know when you say stuff like, *"What more bad can happen?"*
Dear universe — that's sarcasm. It's a joke. It's me having a moment.
It is **not** a challenge.
It is **not** an open invitation to turn my life into an episode of a badly written soap
opera.

But no.
The universe is like that one toxic ex who replies only to the things you wish
they'd ignore and ignores everything you say sincerely.

The universe will ignore 237 'I am worthy' affirmations but immediately act on
that one half-sneeze, half-sulk moment when you muttered, 'I'm so unlucky.'
Boom — noted, stamped, delivered.

So now you're triple-filtering your words, manifesting like a saint, no bad vibes, no F-bombs — just pure, sanitized, spiritual.

And yet, not a damn thing shifted.

You're still staring at the ceiling some nights, asking the universe,
"Bas mujhe hi skip kiya Hai kya?

No villain in your story, no dramatic betrayal.
Just the quiet ache of being overlooked.
Of doing all the "right" things — showing up, being decent, holding space for others —
and still feeling like the only one who is watching everyone else win.

You don't hate them for winning.
You just wish your turn wasn't always *"next season, please stay tuned."*

But you keep going.
Washing your own damn dishes, refilling the water bottle no one touches but you, smiling at weddings where the cake has more tiers than your life plan.

Because you're not jealous.
You're just tired of clapping with hands that have only ever held patience.

And the universe?
Still ghosting you.
Seen. No reply.

One Fine Day, You Give Up

One fine day, you just... give up.

Not in a dramatic, "I'm done with life" way.
Just quietly. Like switching off a light in a room you're not coming back to.

You stop writing affirmations.
You stop pretending the 11:11 wish is going to change anything.
You stop saying "everything happens for a reason" when deep down, you're not even sure if anything's happening at all.

Because you tried. You *really* tried.

You were the good person. The one who kept the faith. Who showed up, even on days you couldn't feel your own heartbeat properly. Who waited, patiently, like something good was on its way.

And the universe?
The universe saw your pain and blinked.

So now?
You don't manifest.
You just sigh. Deep and long. The kind of sigh that carries five years of "maybe tomorrow."

You don't hope. Hope's exhausting.

You just wake up. Check your phone. Brush. Exist.

It's quieter.

You still smile at your coworkers. Still wish your cousin on their engagement. Still pay your Wi-Fi bill.

But inside?
You've muted the universe's chat.

Let it leave you on "read."
You won't be typing anymore.

The Twist

There comes a point when even the most faithful person becomes reluctant with their hope.
Not cynical. Just... careful.
Because hope, when it doesn't land, bruises you from the inside out.

With an unexplainable feeling, call it anger or agony, or may be some big dictionary word.. whatever,
You don't whisper wishes into the ceiling anymore

Instead, you sit with yourself.
You listen to your gut.
And it's awkward at first—like talking to someone you ghosted years ago.
It fumbles, overthinks, second-guesses.
But it doesn't lie to you.

It says: *You're tired.*
It says: *You're doing too much and still feeling like you're not enough. Exhausted.*
Empty.

And then it asks you the question that changes everything:
What if you didn't need the universe to respond?
What if you responded to yourself, first?

You didn't get the job.
You didn't get the person.
You didn't get an apology, or closure, or even an acknowledgment that it hurt.

But you got through this day.
You woke up and brushed your teeth even when everything in you wanted to stay in bed.
You wore clean clothes. You watered your plants. You replied to one unread message.
You smiled at a stranger's child on the street, even though your heart felt like glass.

And in those tiny moments, something subtle but sacred stirs.

Maybe this—
this brutal, silent stretch of life where nothing is promised,
where no higher power hands you anything wrapped in meaning—
is exactly where your resilience is building its quiet little empire.

You're still here.
Still showing up.
Still refusing to turn cold.

Maybe the silence wasn't absence. Maybe it was space — for you to hear yourself.

And maybe the universe isn't punishing you.
Maybe it's waiting for you to become someone who no longer begs for miracles...
May be, the Universe's sign was pointing towards the mirror, which you mistook as 'just' your reflection.

You Were the Sign

The universe wasn't late. It was letting you arrive.

Maybe the silence wasn't rejection.
Maybe it was preparation.

You kept waiting for a miracle —
a sign, a shift, a door flinging open like in the movies.
But all this time, the miracle was you —
unfolding, painfully, beautifully, slowly.

You wanted love?
You were always capable of giving it first.
Unconditional, clumsy, stubborn love — the kind that teaches you
how to hold someone without needing them to stay.

You wanted someone to choose you?
Maybe the lesson was learning how to choose yourself first.
To sit with your fears, your patterns, your wounds —
and still say, "I'm not leaving me this time."

You wanted the job? The breakthrough?
It wasn't just about getting it —
it was about being ready to carry it.

See, growth doesn't announce itself.
It doesn't come with glitter or closure.
It happens quietly — like a vegetable growing out of a flower.
No one claps for it, but that doesn't make it any less valuable.
And the time it takes?
Doesn't change the fact that it's still becoming food,
still becoming worth the harvest.

You weren't abandoned.
You were becoming.
The wait wasn't punishment.
It was proof — that you were worth the time it took.

You were always the sign.
You just needed the silence long enough to see it.

You kept wishing at 11:11 — asking for a better future, hoping the universe would
drop it at your doorstep. But maybe that wish wasn't a shortcut. Maybe it was
a contract. A silent agreement that to *get* the future, you'd have to *build* it. Sow
something. Risk something. Change something. Because the gates don't open just
for want — they open For healing. For heartbreak that softens you. For endurance.
For hard work. For the ugly fights and unlimited chaos and still ending up holding
hands and hope.

So when you made that 11:11 wish for a better life,
the universe heard you.
It just knew you'd have to bleed a little to bloom a lot.

Because the wish wasn't the work.
The waiting wasn't the punishment.
It was preparation.

And turns out —
you weren't being ignored.
You were being *equipped*.

Because anything worth having will test if you're worth holding it.

White Hair? Aging like *fine* guilt...

No one warns you about this stuff. There's no big moment. No epic scene. It always starts in the worst lighting. Not in your cosy bedroom mirror, not in a selfie, not even during a festival photo. You're literally just standing in the bathroom, half awake or half ready and *there it is*.

A strand that stood taller than the rest. Straighter. Bolder. Paler.
White.

At first, you laugh.
Like, "Haha, must be a reflection."
Like you're too young, too *chilled*, too *not married yet yaar* for something like this to happen.

Then, your laugh fades.
Because it's still there. Not light. Not thread. Just... white. Loud white.

Someone inside your head shouts — Wait. If this is here now... does that mean I've crossed *that* line? The invisible one between 'still young' and 'officially adult'?"

Your instinct?
Pluck it out.
Bury the evidence.

But right as your fingers reach for it…
You pause.

Because there's that old superstition your mom once said —
"Don't pull it out. Ten more will come out"

And just like that, a single white strand becomes a horror story in your head.

You're no longer just looking in the mirror.

You're staring into a timeline you didn't approve.

You think of moisturisers you skipped. Sleep you didn't get.
You remember that kid who called you "uncle" last week and you *laughed too hard.*

And suddenly — your reflection isn't about the hair.
It's about the *you* standing behind it.

The version of you that was so busy hustling, healing, planning, pretending —
that you didn't notice when the calendar stopped asking for your opinion.

And that's when it hits you:
This isn't ageing. This is **evidence**.
Of time. Of wear. Of memory.

Your first white hair isn't a crisis.
It's a **notification** —
"Beta, update available. You're not who you used to be."

Hide & Dye

First reaction?
You don't talk about it.
You keep guessing, has everyone seen it, is this why the pretty new intern in the office called you 'Big Bro'?

Then begins the quiet panic.
You part your hair a different way.
You start standing under tube lights at weird angles hoping the reflection hides it.
You zoom in on selfies.

Next: the full research mode.
You're googling in the office washroom —
"Best natural ways to reverse grey hair"
"Grey hair in 20s — is it stress or am I dying?

"Does curry leaves work"

You call your cousin who's doing dermatology.
You message that school friend who once sold herbal shampoo in college.
You ask your mom. She says it's because you are always on the mobile.
You ask your dad. He shrugs and says, "You should rise before 5 am"
[IRRELEVANT]

You binge videos by people who call themselves "Hair Coach" and "Scalp Guru."
One guy says don't use shampoo.
Another says use only shampoo.
Someone else says rub onion juice.

You start checking the back of hair oil bottles in Big Bazaar.
You actually read the ingredients.
You say words like "bhringraj" with a straight face.

You don't trust that weird brown bottle in your bathroom anymore — you want *serum*.
You want *onion extract*.
You want *root activation*.
Even though you don't understand what any of that means.

MAN!

And then… you buy the dye.

You go for the safest shade: *Natural Black.*
Not *Jet Black.* Not *Burgundy.*
You go for something that says, *"I still care, but not desperately."*

You apply it in secret.
Bathroom door locked.
Shirt off.
Plastic gloves on.
Mildly judging yourself the entire time.

And then you wait.
In silence.
For 25 minutes.
Thinking, *"Is this the beginning of maintenance mode?"*

Because now it's not just about hair.
It's about *catching up*.
With your body.
With time.
With how things used to be — and how they look now.

That one strand?
It wasn't grey.
It was honest.
And you weren't ready for the truth.

The Skin Talks Too

You don't notice it until the day you really look.
Like, *really* look.

The puffiness under your eyes —
hasn't gone down in days.
The laugh lines?
Still there long after you stopped laughing.

You run your finger across your cheek and it doesn't bounce back the way it
used to.
Not bad.
Just... different.

And then, this strange thought hits you:
"Did I always look this tired?"

You check old photos.
Zoom in. Zoom out.
Compare jawlines, compare eyes.
You can't tell if it's the lighting or if life's been heavy on your face.

And it's not just the hair anymore.
It's your whole face telling you what your mind's been avoiding:
Something's changed.

Maybe it's age.
Maybe it's late nights.
Or maybe your body's been carrying the emotions you've refused to feel —
and now it's just showing them.

Because the body remembers.
Every unfinished conversation.
Every fake smile.
Every sleepless night.

And now your face wears it all.
Nothing loud.
Nothing tragic.
Just the slow, soft erosion that happens
when you survive instead of heal.

And suddenly, a little grey hair feels like the least of your truths.

Trophy or Threat?

You've survived enough to be proud.

But

You look in the mirror a second longer. You feel like someone hit fast-forward without asking.

Everyone says aging is beautiful. You've got more clarity, fewer friends. More money, less excitement. You've grown. You're stable. You've stopped chasing nonsense.

BUT
It's also confusing. It makes you question stuff you thought you had figured out.

You try to balance everything — career, health, family, some vague passion project you started in 2019.

But something inside quietly asks,
"Is my best already behind me?"

A small part of you misses the chaos.
The recklessness.
The not knowing.

You take pride in how far you've come.
But sometimes...
you're scared you'll never feel that *alive* again.

This age — this grey strand — it doesn't ask you to panic. It just tells you, "It's time."

Time to let go of guilt.

Guilt isn't just feeling bad — it's feeling responsible for things you never had control over, and punishing yourself for it, quietly, every day.

Guilt of not being enough, not doing enough, not becoming who your parents dreamt, not calling enough, not earning enough, not settling down fast enough.

And no, it doesn't just sit quietly in a corner of your mind.
It shows up in your body.

In fatigue you can't explain.
In hair that grays faster than it should.
In skin that loses glow, not from age — but from carrying shame.
In the way your jaw clenches every time someone says, "You should've…"

The Fear is-

Where we'd left behind the *basic maintenance of our mind.*
Where we carried guilt like vitamins, and forgot to take actual ones.
Where we abused sleep, skipped water, laughed less, and stressed more.

We weren't afraid of growing old.
We were afraid of discovering how badly we treated the person we were growing into.

It *reminds* us — of how little care we've given ourselves.

But here's the thing: grey hair isn't a warning. It can be a beginning.Because youth isn't skin-deep. It's energy-deep. It's about choosing to live — not just to be alive.

Grey doesn't mean old.
Wrinkles don't mean worn out.
It only starts feeling old when you start **living like you've got nothing left to look forward to.**

So yeah—
Grey hair can be sexy.
Saggy skin can be beautiful.
The only thing that's not beautiful?
Turning your entire life grey before it's even done.

Lessons Learnt Outside the Syllabus

Your teacher once made you memorize the structure of the heart.
But no one told you what to do when it breaks.
You studied the parts — atrium, ventricle, valves — but no one said anything about loneliness. Or watching your parents fight and pretending not to hear.

They said "remember this," so you did.
Not because it made sense.
But because you were scared of being called "slow."
Because getting things right in school was the only place you didn't feel wrong.

You learned how to draw the digestive system — liver, stomach, intestines.
But no one taught you how to digest disappointment.
You failed a test once and the silence at dinner felt like punishment.
You topped another and everyone acted like peace had returned.

That was your first lesson in *conditional love.*
And no, it wasn't in the textbook.

You were told how to fill answer sheets.
Not how to fill the silence when your best friend suddenly stops texting you.
Not how to stop chasing people who treat you like an optional subject.

You could recite poems. You still remember *"The Road Not Taken."*
But nobody told you that whichever road you take,
you'll carry your past like an old school bag — heavy, half-torn, full of things you never needed.

They said, *"Life is the real exam."*
Turns out, they were right.
But they forgot to mention that there's no syllabus.
No grace marks.
And that half the time, you're not even sure which question you're trying to answer.

You weren't taught that your parents were once kids too,
that they didn't grow up with therapy or self-help books.
That maybe they did their best.
That their love came wrapped in guilt, fear, *aur thoda sa taunt bhi.*

You were never told that "success" might make you feel more alone, not less.
That "achievers" also cry in the shower.
That you could meet every expectation and still feel like you've let everyone down.

And now, years later, you find yourself
with a polished resume, decent salary, and a quiet ache
you can't quite explain.

No one prepared you for this part.
For the part where you're successful on paper
but emotionally homeless.

They taught us how to solve equations, but forgot to mention people don't come
with formulas.
You can be perfectly polite, emotionally available, and kind —
and still be the one ghosted, overlooked, or blamed.

Because life isn't a moral science class.
And being nice? That's not extra credit. It's just... expected.

Being Nice Is Not a Guarantee Card

You can be the warmest damn blanket in the world,
and someone will still say you're suffocating them.

You were taught — at home, in school, in that overhyped motivational webinar —
that being kind, polite, and soft-spoken will open doors.
Turns out, some of those doors lead straight to manipulation, gaslighting, or
unpaid internships.

You smiled through that uncomfortable group project,
helped *Riya* with her assignment even though she once stole your pen *and your
crush,*
gave your friend a birthday gift even when they forgot yours — twice.
And what did you get?
Left on read. Emotionally overdrafted. And the eternal label of *"so sweet yaar."*

No one warns you that *"so sweet"* is just Indian for *"walk all over me, I won't complain."*

You assumed people would mirror your kindness.
Instead, you became the friend who's always available,
the colleague who gets dumped extra work with a *"you're so efficient yaar,"*
the partner who's loved *mostly* for their patience,
and then blamed for being *too emotional* the one time you cracked.

Here's the truth:
Being nice doesn't guarantee closure.
It doesn't promise reciprocation.
It sure as hell doesn't prevent betrayal.

But the worst part?
You still keep trying.
Because somewhere deep inside,
you believe that if you're just *nicer*, more *understanding*, less *you*,
they'll finally stay. Finally love you right.

And then, one day, you realize…
you were never too much.
You were just too available for people who never knew what to do with enough.

You'll remember this when your phone lights up,
and your thumb hesitates over a "Sure, no problem."
You'll still say yes.
But it'll feel different. Heavier.

Because now you know —
kindness is free, but it can cost you your self-respect.

And that's when it hits you — being kind doesn't come with a receipt. Being the bigger person? That just means you get hit harder. Loyalty isn't noble, it's risky. And no, the universe doesn't keep a scoreboard.

You grew up thinking life was a classroom. Turns out it's more like a moving train with no seatbelts and everyone yelling that it's your turn to drive.

And still, you keep showing up — with a cracked voice, a tired smile, and the emotional energy of a phone on 1% battery.

Closure Is a Luxury Item

Some people leave like they're late for a train — sudden, unannounced, no goodbye, no forwarding address. Just gone.

No fight. No closure. Just an eerie silence that echoes louder than a scream.
And the worst part? You still check your phone like they might explain.
They don't.
They never will.

It could be a friend — the one who knew your family secrets, saw you cry at your lowest, and still managed to gossip about you.
It could be the person who said they'd stay. The one who made you believe in softness, only to turn cold.
Or maybe it's someone who pretended to be kind just long enough to see how far you'd bend.

They didn't slam the door.
They just quietly disappeared — and left you to mop up the mess of a storm they created.
You thought love, or loyalty, or decency meant they'd at least say goodbye.
But some people only enter your life to teach you how to survive without an apology.

And here's the truth nobody told you in school:
Closure is a luxury item.
You can't afford to wait for it.
You give it to yourself.

You stop rereading the last conversation.
You stop thinking if you were "too much" or "not enough."
You bury the version of you that still believes they'll come back with answers.

….*'I used to think people leave because I wasn't enough. Now I know — they needed to meet themselves, and I was just standing on the way. And if they couldn't stop for themselves, I shouldn't have stayed for them either.'*

You'll Break Before You Bend

Because sometimes, the people who held your hand the longest are the ones who taught you how to live without one.

It's not the heartbreak that bruises the deepest — it's the confusion.

They smiled.
They hugged.
They said they loved you, or maybe they just said "yaar, always with you." And they meant it, until they didn't.

They knew your wounds and still decided to bleed you dry.

And the worst part?
You didn't see it coming. You didn't *want* to.

You defended them in rooms they laughed about you in.
You stood up for them when they were sitting down on your name.
You believed in second chances while they were busy preparing your last one.

But betrayal doesn't announce itself with lightning and thunder.
It shows up on a normal Thursday. In a forwarded message. A story tag. A conversation you weren't meant to hear.

And then it grows roots inside your chest.
You question your judgment, your memory, your worth.
Were you too trusting? Too naïve? Too... *you*?

You don't break because of what they did.
You break because of what you *thought* they'd never do.

And after the crying stops, and your fists unclench, and your voice finally learns to say their name without trembling —
you realise: you're still here.

You may be bleeding.
But you're still breathing.

And that's the real miracle:
Not that they left.
But that you didn't leave yourself behind trying to understand why.

Sometimes, closure doesn't come wrapped in apology or regret.
Sometimes, it's just a quiet decision to never look back.
To keep walking with the limp.
To still show up, gentler — but wiser.

Healing Isn't Graded, Either

You don't get a certificate for keeping it together when everything inside you was screaming.
There's no prize money for learning how to sit through the ache without texting the person who caused it.

Most healing doesn't look brave — it looks boring.
It looks like sleeping on time. Like saying no to people who confuse your kindness with free labor.
Like unfollowing them even though a small part of you still hopes they'll miss you.

We were taught to chase medals and grades — measurable wins.
But real life? It claps for you in silence.
And some days, it doesn't clap at all.

You realize healing is not a graph that always goes up.
It's not linear, it's not public, and it's definitely not pretty.
One day you're fine, the next day a song ruins your evening.
You cry. You scroll. You make tea.
That's progress, too.

And here's the gut-punch:
Some people won't say sorry.
Some won't even realize they hurt you.
You won't get closure — you'll get tired.
And you'll walk away because peace is more useful than being right.

Eventually, you stop waiting for them to fix what they broke.
You stop sending out emotional invoices no one ever intended to pay.
You stop being the rehab centre for people who were just tourists in your life.

That's what healing actually is.
Not becoming invincible — but becoming unavailable to bullshit.

And no one's going to give you a medal for it.
But one day, you'll notice:
Your body breathes easier.
You laugh without guilt.
You don't rehearse conversations in your head anymore.

And that… is enough.

Life doesn't hand out report cards, just scars in places no one can see. But it teaches you anyway—brutally, beautifully—and if you're still standing, that's your A grade.

Still Trying to Figure It Out

I used to think one day I'd wake up and feel... done.
I mean settled kind of - done.
Like someone who had figured out the difference between peace and just being numb.
Like I'd crossed some invisible finish line and was finally standing at the version of me I was always supposed to become.

But life doesn't work like that.

There's no moment when it all clicks.
There are just scattered minutes—somewhere between folding clothes and crying on auto rides—where you realize you're not who you were.
And that's something.

We grow in half-sleeves and heartbreaks.
In awkward silences and late-night overthinking.
In the "I'm fine" texts we send when we're anything but.

The truth is, there's no arrival.
No big ceremony that says, *"You made it."*
Just tiny wins.
Small shifts.
And the quiet pride of surviving one more day with your kindness intact.

So no, I haven't arrived.
But I'm still here. Still walking.
And maybe that counts more than any finish line ever could.

But just when I start making peace with where I am—
the ghosts of "where I should've been" come knocking.

Haunted by Should-Haves

I should've been married by now.
Or at least engaged. Or in a situationship serious enough to ruin my sleep cycle.

I should've had a savings plan. A skincare routine. A gym membership I actually use.
I should've known how to cook something other than Maggi without watching a YouTube tutorial like it's rocket science.

And maybe...
I should've healed.
From that one heartbreak. That one fight. That one version of me who never spoke up, never said no, never asked for the things I really wanted.

But instead, I'm here—still using sarcasm to hide panic attacks, still crying at shampoo ads for no reason, and still pretending I don't Google "how to feel less lost" at 2 AM.
The "should-haves" are relentless.
They don't knock—they barge in.
While you're brushing your teeth or scrolling reels or just trying to exist without comparing yourself to someone who bought a house at 25.

We carry this invisible pressure-
We should be further.
We should be better.
We should be over it by now.

But what if the "should" is just noise?

What if healing takes longer than 10 Instagram slides?
What if growth doesn't look like glow-ups and checklists, but like slowly not hating yourself for needing more time?

Because honestly, some of us didn't get a head start.
Some of us were just trying to survive while others were learning to thrive.
Some of us were breaking cycles, while others were just buying cycles on EMI.

So yeah—
I didn't become who I was *supposed* to be.
But maybe that version was never meant for me.

Maybe becoming *this me*—scarred, slow, soft, and still trying—
was always the point.

And if that makes me late to the party, so be it.

Besides, the ones who show up late usually bring the best stories.

Learning to Sit With Yourself

Let's be honest—being alone with your thoughts?
It's weird.
Uncomfortable.
Sometimes, straight-up scary.

We'll do anything to avoid it.
Play music while we shower. Watch reels while we eat. Scroll through five people's heartbreak before even brushing our teeth.

Because when everything goes quiet,
your brain starts talking.

It reminds you of things you didn't want to think about—
the argument you avoided,
the message you never replied to,
that one sentence someone said in 2014 that still makes your chest feel weird.

So instead, we go online.
And social media—God bless it—has advice for *everything*.

"If your parents ignored your tears, you were an unloved child."
And you read that like,
*Oh… sh*t. That's me.

But slow down.
Is it?

Were you unloved?

Look, it's not that those posts are wrong.
It's that they don't know *your* full story.
They can't.
They weren't there during your birthday when your dad didn't say much but gave you money to buy whatever you wanted, instead of replacing the pair of shoes he has been wearing for more than half a decade now.

We're so quick to believe a sentence from a stranger on the internet.
But we don't sit back and weigh the full picture.
What they gave. What they failed at. What they didn't know how to say.
We don't reflect. We react.

Sitting with yourself means doing the uncomfortable thing—
asking, *What's true for me?*
Not what gets likes.
Not what sounds woke.
Not what rhymes well on a reel.

It means realising some things hurt... but they weren't cruel.
Some people loved you... not just the way internet showed us, but in their own way. OWN UNIQUE WAY.
And some memories need clarity, not a viral quote.

So no, don't believe everything you see.
But also—don't ignore what you feel.
Somewhere in between what's said and what's unsaid... is you.

Messy, sometimes too forgiving, sometimes too hard on yourself.
But real. And worth knowing.

And here's the thing- once you *really* sit with yourself—no distractions, no performances—something strange starts to happen:
you start... figuring things out.

Figuring Out

Nobody tells you this, but the first time you really start figuring yourself out...
it doesn't feel wise.
It feels *scary as hell.*

It's like someone suddenly turned on all the lights in a room you didn't know you were living in. And now you're staring at all the emotional clutter you'd shoved under the bed—old fears, quiet anger, forgotten memories, survival habits...

You notice things that were always there, just... blurred out.

That you flinch at love.
That you confuse peace with boredom.
That praise makes you feel nervous, not happy—because deep down, you don't believe it.

No one prepares you for how disorienting it is to realise you've been functioning on autopilot—doing things, saying things, loving people—not because you *chose* to, but because you were wired that way a long time ago.

And for a while, it messes with you.
You start questioning everything.
Was that really love?
Did I actually want that, or did I just think I was supposed to?
Am I angry at them, or at myself?

It's uncomfortable.
It's lonely.
You start noticing patterns, but you don't always know what to do with them.

Like—
Why do I freeze when someone asks what I want?
Why do I apologise when I cry?
Why do I keep trying to be 'low-maintenance' in a world that doesn't even refill the emotional tank?

And then, slowly, one messy realisation at a time...
you begin to understand.

You're not broken.
You're just responding to things that happened before you had words for them.
Your coping isn't weakness—it's evidence that you survived things no one saw.

Figuring out isn't a glow-up. It is a kind of humour that feels like a smirk between tears. A "yeah, I'm healing, but I still check if my ex viewed my story"
It's more like... an emotional excavation.
You dig, you uncover, you sit with things.
And sometimes you cry in the middle of making Maggi because a memory hit you too hard, too fast.

But the beautiful part?

Once you see a pattern, you can choose something different.
You can say no where you used to stay silent.
You can feel sad without calling yourself dramatic.
You can say, *"That hurt me"* without explaining why or apologising for it.

Figuring out isn't finishing the puzzle.
It's realising you *are* the puzzle.

And finally sitting down to understand how all your pieces fit—crooked, weird, beautiful, and true.

You're not done.
But you're not lost anymore either.

Becoming Me, Anyway

After all the overthinking, panic googling, crying in Ola cabs, long lectures from relatives, growing up too fast, hiding pain under "haan haan sab theek hai," career pressure, low battery friendships, and suddenly realising even *you* don't know what you're doing... you finally get it, a little.

You don't get everything in life.
You're not supposed to.
And honestly, most of us are just pretending we've got it sorted.
And maybe that's fine.

Some people have beautiful families.
Some people have friends who are basically family.
Some find love young.
Some keep falling for emotionally unavailable people.

Some people heal fast.
Some people write sad captions and pretend it's poetry.
Some laugh louder now because they cried quietly for years.

Some people wake up feeling healed.
Some need two alarms and a 10-minute cry in the bathroom before facing the world.

And you—
You're somewhere in between.
Too old to keep blaming life.
Too young to have it all figured out.
Too tired to pretend.
Too hopeful to give up. Some days, you laugh too loud at reels that aren't even funny.
Other days, you just stare at your fan, blankly, hoping the spinning will untangle your thoughts too, swinging between *"I'm okay"* and *"What is happening to me?"*

You thought by now you'd have answers.
Or at least some kind of balance.
But instead, you've got unread messages, missed calls, half-finished plans, and a
body that's been trying to talk to you for years.

Through that constant fatigue you call "normal."
Through the sudden chest tightness you explain away as acidity.
Through the way your shoulders never really relax anymore.

And the worst part?
You almost got used to it.
To ignoring yourself.
To calling survival "strength."
To brushing off your own needs like they're a luxury you can't afford.

And then Something shifted.
Quietly, without warning.

And that's when it begins.
Not with a quote or a reel or a sudden spiritual awakening.
But with a quiet decision—
To stop abandoning yourself.

You start paying attention.
To the lump in your throat during dinner.
To the way your chest feels after a phone call.
To how much peace costs in this world of constant noise.

And when you finally start recognising yourself—
not the version people like, but the version that wakes up with you—
everything shifts a little.

You begin learning.
Not perfectly, not all at once.
But slowly.
You learn that resting isn't laziness.
That not replying doesn't mean you're selfish.
That outgrowing people isn't betrayal—it's biology.
That your worth has nothing to do with your productivity.
And love…
It doesn't have to be loud to be real.
It just has to feel safe.

You stop waiting for someone to validate your healing.
You stop trying to be "normal" again.
You start choosing yourself in small, quiet ways.
A soft "no."
A walk alone.
Sitting with discomfort instead of escaping it.

And eventually, you stop apologising for who you're becoming.
Because this version of you?
The one who's still figuring it out but shows up anyway?
They're not broken.
They're just... real.

And that's powerful.

You're not who you were.
Not yet who you'll be.
But right now?

You're finally, fully, without anyone's consent
Becoming you (unapologetically).

Still Becoming...

So... here you are.
The last page.
The quiet after the storm of underlines, nods, sighs, and maybe even a tear or two you pretended was "just allergies."

You didn't just read a book — you walked through your own thoughts. Sat with emotions you often rush past. Looked at your reflection not to judge it, but to understand it.

And if there's one thing I want you to carry with you, it's this:

You are not a problem to solve.
You are not behind.
You are not a late bloomer or a lost cause.
You are a life in motion.

Despite what the world sometimes screams — there is no timeline that defines your worth. No checklist that confirms you're doing okay. No applause that can substitute for inner peace. Progress looks different on everyone — and often, it looks nothing like what we imagined.

Some days, healing is loud and victorious.
Some days, it's just getting out of bed. Or replying to one text. Or forgiving yourself for not being as "productive" as you thought you'd be by now.

Still becoming means learning that your value isn't in how much you achieve, but in how deeply you live — with honesty, softness, and a willingness to begin again.

So even when life feels blurry, and everyone else seems ten steps ahead...
Even when you're questioning everything, and motivation feels like a stranger...
Even then — especially then — you are still becoming.

And that's more than enough.

Close this book gently. Let the words settle.
Take what stays with you. Let go of what doesn't.
Then go live — imperfectly, courageously, and in your own unique rhythm.

Cheers to your messy, honest, quietly brave progress.

Love from a heart that's still figuring it out,

Sruti